THE FOURTH GOSPEL AND THE LATER EPISTLES

JOHN KNOX

ABINGDON PRESS
New York ● *Nashville*

THE FOURTH GOSPEL AND THE LATER EPISTLES

Copyright MCMXLV by Whitmore & Stone

J

SET UP, PRINTED, AND BOUND BY THE
PARTHENON PRESS, AT NASHVILLE,
TENNESSEE, UNITED STATES OF AMERICA

TO

AMOS
Good old friend

And to the Memory of

HIS FATHER
Who was my father's friend

EDITOR'S PREFACE

THIS volume is intended to help the reader who wishes to know the Bible at first hand. The way to know a country is to visit it and travel through it, not just to read about it. But a good guide can help. He can lead to places of greatest interest and can give information needed for understanding what is seen. The Bible is a great and wonderful country. It is not one book but many books—books in which many voices join, and whose story stretches through many centuries. Its writings differ widely in character, as do the mountains and valleys, the rivers and seacoasts, the cities and plains, of a wide country like ours. At the same time, they have a real unity. They have one source, the Spirit of God moving upon the hearts of men. They have a living center, Jesus of Nazareth. We call the Bible the Word of God, and with good reason, for it comes out of the word which God spoke to these writers "by divers portions and in divers manners," and through it God speaks to us today.

All of us know some parts of the Bible quite well—a chapter here, a verse there, certain psalms learned perhaps in childhood, and some parts of the New Testament. But we all need wider acquaintance with the Bible, and truer understanding and larger appreciation of its wealth of moral and spiritual meaning.

This book is one of eight Guides planned for the purpose of leading to this broader knowledge. The authors have been chosen because of their training in Bible study and their experience in teaching. Four of the books are given to the Old Testament, four to the New. Many of the less important parts of the Bible have of necessity been omitted. The Guides go with the reader on his journey through these writings. They stimulate interest and understanding. They introduce the writer and indicate the time, place, purpose, and special character of the writing. Chapter by chapter, they help the student to discover the meanings and values in the Bible, especially for the personal religious life. Since these Guides will be used largely by ministers, attention is given to material for sermons; but the lay reader will find them equally helpful. Each book is intended to serve for a six months' period. Four or five *Readings* should be completed each week.

Here are some *rules for Bible reading* whose observance will pay rich dividends:

1. Read with a definite purpose and expectation: to understand what is written; to gain quickening of thought and enlargement of mind and vision; to get personal help for good living; and, above all, to meet God and to hear his voice. These are great ends; whether they are reached will rest with each student.

2. Bring all that you have to your reading. What you get will depend on what you bring. Especially, bring a sympathetic imagination. You will not be reading dead words. They came out of life. Try to enter into that life of the past: into the faith of a psalmist and his trials and hopes, the appeal of a prophet speaking to a nation, the witness of Paul, the full heart of the Evangelists. Occasional reading aloud will help make the words live. Bring also an attentive and inquiring mind. Read slowly, pause, reflect, always seeking the real meaning.

3. Read in the spirit of prayer. Offer a prayer as you begin. Ask for the light which God's Spirit can give. Lift up your heart to God and ask God to come to you.

4. Read in the spirit of obedience. Ask what the passage means for your own life and pray for grace to follow what is thus revealed. "Apply thyself wholly to the Bible; apply the Bible wholly to thyself." (Bengel.)

EDITOR'S PREFACE

In this course are frequent references to *ABC,* which means *The Abingdon Bible Commentary,* a commentary on the Old and New Testaments which contains many interesting articles on the Bible as a whole as well as an article on each book of the Bible. The purchase of this book is recommended to the lay reader, who will find it most interesting and helpful. For the minister who is studying these Guides it is indispensable.

The student will find that keeping a notebook from day to day as he reads will prove of great value.

HARRIS FRANKLIN RALL

FOREWORD

THE general purpose of this book has been stated in the Editor's Preface. I gladly associate myself with this purpose and hope that the following pages may do their proper part in fulfilling it. The book presumes to be neither Introduction nor Commentary, but enough of each to be helpful.

The biblical books treated are divided into approximately a hundred *Readings,* and it is recommended that one of these be done each day. I have divided my treatment of each *Reading* into two parts: numbered instructions and questions, followed by comments, with a request for "Written Work" after each six or seven *Readings.*

My suggestion as to method of study is this: (1) Read the biblical passage indicated. (2) Give attention to the "Instructions and Questions." (3) Read the "Comments." (4) Read through the biblical passage again. (5) Do the "Written Work" if any is assigned.

The student may advantageously read the selected biblical passage in one of the new translations—such as Goodspeed's or Moffatt's—as well as in a standard version. And it is hoped he will not limit his reading of *The Abingdon Bible Commentary* to passages specifically recommended.

For further study of the problems of introduction which these books of the New Testament involve, the reader is referred to any of the recent excellent Introductions. The following, among many others, can be recommended as reliable and nontechnical: E. J. Goodspeed, *An Introduction to the New Testament;* M. S. Enslin, *Christian Beginnings;* E. F. Scott, *The Literature of the New Testament;* C. T. Craig, *The Beginning of Christianity.*

11

THE FOURTH GOSPEL AND THE LATER EPISTLES

For further special study of the several New Testament books the student is referred to the literature mentioned at the end of the introductory articles in *ABC*. I shall occasionally suggest additions to these lists.

I am grateful to Harper & Brothers for permission to quote occasionally from James Moffatt, *The Bible: A New Translation,* and from G. H. C. Macgregor, *The Gospel of John;* to the University of Chicago Press for permission to make occasional use of E. J. Goodspeed, *The New Testament: An American Translation;* to The Macmillan Company for permission to quote several times from R. H. Strachan, *The Fourth Gospel: Its Significance and Environment;* and to Charles Scribner's Sons for permitting quotations from E. F. Scott, *The Fourth Gospel: Its Purpose and Theology,* and from F. C. Burkitt, *The Gospel History and Its Transmission.*

I cannot begin adequately to acknowledge my indebtedness to these and other students of the New Testament. I have done very little "spade work" in the part of the New Testament literature dealt with in this volume, and have therefore been more than ordinarily dependent upon the researches and suggestions of others. I have tried to give credit where direct dependence upon a published work is involved; but I do not doubt that some cases of this kind have been missed. So far as the Gospel of John is concerned, besides to Macgregor, Strachan, and Scott, I owe a special debt to my friend Ernest C. Colwell, of the University of Chicago. In the discussion of the Pastoral Epistles I am at many points indebted to another friend, Martin Rist, of the Iliff School of Theology. My indebtedness to some of the writers of *ABC* is, I suppose, to be taken for granted, given the particular character and purpose of this volume and its relation to that Commentary; but I am glad to acknowledge my obligation, nevertheless.

JOHN KNOX

Union Theological Seminary
New York City

12

CONTENTS

INTRODUCTION

THE twenty-seven books of the N.T. can be classified in various ways. One of the most frequent methods of classification arranges them in three groups: the Letters of Paul, the Synoptic Gospels and Acts, and the "Later Books." These "later books," like the "Writings" of the O.T. canon, are a rather miscellaneous category, containing Revelation, Hebrews, the fourth Gospel, the Catholic Epistles (James; 1 and 2 Peter; 1, 2, and 3 John; Jude), and the Pastoral Epistles (1 and 2 Timothy and Titus). Of these, Revelation has been dealt with in a previous book in this series. The present volume is an invitation to read the rest of these later books. They are in many ways the most interesting books in the N.T.

Something may appropriately be said about these books as a group before we turn to read them severally. The most important thing to note about them is that they reflect the life and thought of the Christian churches in the period, roughly, between 95 and 150 A.D. This fact is important not only for our understanding of these documents but also for our knowledge of the church during that period. Indeed, much the greater part of what we know about Christianity in the last decade of the first century and the first half of the second is derived from these books.

A short account of the purpose of each will be given as we begin our reading in each case. We shall see that the occasions which called forth the several documents were varied and complex. It may be said, however, that in general two necessities tend to dominate Christian writing in this period: (1) the necessity of preparing the churches to withstand persecution, and (2) the necessity of keeping the faith of the church free from heretical error and distortion. A few words about each of these interests will help us approach this group of books with greater understanding.

Let us consider, first, the matter of persecution. Christianity began its course in Palestine, where it was undoubtedly the object of considerable Jewish opposition. Jesus had been put to death by the Romans, rather than by the Jews; but there can be little question that he had incurred the hostility of powerful groups among his countrymen, just as he would incur hostility among us if he should appear in the same way again. After his death, the little group of his disciples, who went about preaching that he was the promised Messiah, that he had risen from the dead and would come again soon to judge the nation and the world—this group had little success among orthodox Jews; indeed, there is every indication of growing unpopularity, if not of actual persecution.

This opposition on the part of the orthodox community was owing partly, no doubt, to outrage that a man crucified by the Romans should be proclaimed the King and Saviour of Israel, but more to disapproval of some practices of the early Christians. There was a tendency on the part of many of the believers to relax the ceremonial requirements of Judaism; this disregard of the Law in some cases went as far as complete table fellowship with non-Jews. This was intolerable to the strict Jew, who saw in such laxness a threat to the whole way of life which alone enabled the Jew to resist the paganism which pressed in so powerfully from all sides.

But whatever the causes, there can be no doubt of the fact of Jewish opposition, first in Palestine and later wherever the evangelists and missionaries went. It must soon have appeared to Paul and other early leaders that the future of the new movement—at least, its immediate future—lay among Gentiles, who in increasing numbers were being reached by the preaching and brought into the churches.

So far as pagans generally were concerned, the Christians

16

in the very beginning would have been looked upon as a Jewish sect; and, however unpopular they may have been on that account, there would have been no legal or state-directed persecution. Religions in Roman society had to be licensed; the government was very suspicious of a new religion, fearing that it was a mere "cover" for a seditious or revolutionary movement. Judaism was a licensed, well-established religion, and as long as the believers in Christ were regarded as belonging to that religion—either as born Jews or as proselytes—the state took no cognizance of them. The Jews, of course, "knew better"; they knew not only that this group was not truly Jewish but also that it was undermining the very foundations of Judaism, all the while benefiting from the immunity which Judaism enjoyed. No wonder hostility of synagogue to church grew! But during this period the state was a friend rather than an enemy; it protected the church against these Jewish attacks (see Acts 18:12f.).

This confusion could not last long, however, and by the end of the first century—the period of the "later books"—it had become clear to Roman governors and magistrates that Christianity was really a new, and therefore an illicit, faith. At first there was no systematic persecution. Action against Christians was taken locally, and much depended upon local conditions as to what kind of action was taken or whether any action at all was taken. There are many reasons for supposing, for example, that there was a vigorous persecution of Christians in the province of Asia (see last map in *ABC*) in the nineties; and one of Pliny's letters (quoted on pp. 108f.) lets us know that twenty years later prosecutions of Christians were taking place in Pontus and Bithynia, where he was governor (see map again). There were many other cases of this kind. But determined attempts on an empire-wide scale to extirpate Christianity, such as the attempt under Decius about 250 A.D., did not occur in the N.T. period.

Still, persecution was even then a constant threat and often broke upon the church in a particular region with hellish fury. To be a Christian was a capital offense; and if it was according to one's conscience or for any reason to one's interest to denounce a man or woman to the authorities as a Christian, it was the Roman official's duty to investigate and punish. And if the official himself had strong feelings in the matter he might at any time make a bold effort to stamp out the religion in his territory.

Our sympathy with the victims of this policy must not blind us to the grounds for the policy from the Roman's point of view. In his view, the safety and prosperity of the Roman state depended upon the favor of the gods of the state; and that favor in turn depended upon the sincere, regular, and general observance of the ordained rites of worship. But the Christians did not participate in or support this worship; on the contrary, they openly declared that the gods of the state had no existence and encouraged citizens generally to disregard their obligations to them. From the point of view of a patriotic and pious Roman, therefore, Christians were a real peril to the state. There were often other less worthy reasons for persecution, but it is well to see how one of the more intelligent and responsible Roman officials might have looked on the growth of the church. Pliny's letter is enlightening at this point.

Now obviously this constant danger of persecution and the not infrequent outbreaks of it posed a terrible problem for the Christian leader. The people must be prepared and encouraged to stand firm in the face of persecution and under it. As we shall see, much in the later books of the N.T. is designed to give this preparation and encouragement. Hebrews and 1 Peter, not to mention Revelation, are dominated by this interest, but it appears somewhat in almost all of them.

About the danger of heresy I can speak more briefly. Everything indicates that in the church, down to 150 A.D., there was great variety of doctrinal belief. The Apostles' Creed had not been formulated; certainly nothing like it had been generally adopted. But, even so, by the end of the first century there had appeared certain theological tendencies which many church leaders recognized as unsound and dangerous. For example, there was the belief that matter was essentially evil and that Christ, therefore, could not have come in the flesh. This was called "Docetism," from the word meaning "to seem"—Christ only "seemed" to be human. Often related to this belief—especially in a powerful movement called Marcionism—was the view that this world had not been created by God the Father, but by another and inferior God. The true and highest God was revealed for the first time in Christ. This God, far from having anything to do with the making of this world, had sent Christ to redeem us from it. Those who held this conception were likely to think of Judaism as the religion of the Creator—rather than of the Father—God and to repudiate the O.T. as belonging only to that religion.

Such tendencies, along with others we shall notice, characterized a general movement of religious life and thought commonly referred to as "Gnosticism." These tendencies reached their flower only in the second century, but they were present in the latter part of the first. Many Christian teachers recognized the error and the danger to the unity of the church which lay in them. The Johannine Epistles, for example, are very much concerned about Docetism, as we shall see, and the Pastoral Epistles about Marcionism. But most of the "later books" are in some measure involved in the fight against various forms of Gnostic doctrine.

The chronological order of the books which we shall read cannot be determined with absolute precision. I should be inclined to place them tentatively as follows: Hebrews, 1 Peter, James, the Gospel of John, the Epistles of John, 1 and 2 Timothy and Titus, Jude and 2 Peter. Because of its unique importance among these books, we shall read the Gospel of John first. The other books we shall take up in the order indicated.

This little volume is proposed as an invitation and a guide, not as an attempt at adequate interpretation. The books of the N.T. must, in the last resort, speak their own message to our minds and hearts.

I

THE GOSPEL OF JOHN

ALTHOUGH it was not written till 100 A.D. or later, the Gospel of John has had from the beginning an enormous influence. For the understanding of the development of theology in the primitive church, there can be no doubt that the important names are Paul, Mark, and John; and the extent to which the devotional and sacramental life of the church has been nourished by this Gospel is beyond any possible calculation.

It is not my purpose to write an adequate introduction to the Gospel. The reader will have beside him *ABC*, which contains an admirable introduction by Principal Garvie. No book in the Bible presents more difficult questions of interpretation, and complete agreement among scholars is not to be expected; but Garvie's statement is at the main points trustworthy, and the reader of these pages will do well to familiarize himself with it. Acquaintance with pp. 1060-66 of *ABC* will be assumed in what follows.

In this brief discussion some of the usual questions of introduction can be summarily dealt with. As to date, I have said that the Gospel cannot have been earlier than 100 A.D., and it can now be added that MS. and other evidence will prevent our dating it later than 150 A.D., or a little before. As to place of writing, there is no sufficient reason to question the traditional ascription of the Gospel to Ephesus, although Alexandria in Egypt has often been seriously proposed. As to audience, nothing is more certain than that the book was intended for Greek, not Jewish, readers.

21

THE FOURTH GOSPEL AND THE LATER EPISTLES

As to authorship, the view that the Gospel could have been written by John, the son of Zebedee, has been all but universally abandoned. Many—for example, Garvie—believe that another John, referred to in Christian writing of the early second century as "the Elder," was the author; but that position is precarious. It is safer to say that we do not know the name of the author, although we can gather a great deal about his personality from the pages of his book. Some who agree that John the disciple did not write the book are nevertheless convinced that the author had access to eye-witness testimony. A few of those who take this position think that this "Witness," who stands back of the writer, was John the disciple; others, like Garvie, think it more probable that this Witness was some Jerusalemite disciple of Jesus whose name we do not know. We can know him only as the Gospel presents him: "the disciple whom Jesus loved." Garvie's distinction between "Witness," "Evangelist," and "Redactor" (see *ABC*, p. 1065a) would be concurred in by some scholars and dissented from by others. On these matters agreement is not to be expected. The important thing is to recognize that this Gospel took form on Gentile soil to meet the needs of Gentile churches. This brings us to the topic which we must consider at somewhat greater length, the purpose of the Gospel.

One who without previous knowledge of the Gospels came directly from a reading of Mark, Matthew, and Luke to the fourth Gospel would be startled at once by the most remarkable differences. We are so familiar with the Gospels as a whole and so accustomed to harmonizing one Gospel with the others that we are not ordinarily aware of these differences.

Most remarkable, perhaps, are the omissions. Professor C. R. Bowen points out that the author of the fourth Gospel nowhere uses

the words pity, mercy, compassion, nor suggests the quality; nowhere brings in the poor (only 12:5f.) or the rich; nowhere a publican, a sinner, a widow. a child, a scribe, a Sadducee; no-

22

where mentions any of the Herods, or Gentiles; no Tyre or Sidon, no Mount of Olives; no unclean demoniacs or reference to their cleansing; no repentance and no forgiveness of sin, neither the words nor the ideas; no *prayer* or praying ("ask" and "beg" occur), no *gospel*, no *preaching*, no *apostle* (the word in 13:16 is in another sense); no faith, no hope, no wisdom [that is, these *words* do not appear]; no *parable,* and, most amazingly, no Kingdom of God (3:3-5 being the one exception).[1]

Dr. Ernest C. Colwell, to whom I am indebted for this quotation, goes on to say:

To this list it may be added that in John there is no genealogy, no birth of Jesus, no birth of the Baptist, no wise men or shepherds, or flight to Egypt, no slaughter of the innocents, no visit of the boy Jesus to the temple, no actual baptism of Jesus, no future judgment (except vestigial survivals), no second Messianic coming, no room for Pentecost, no sons of Zebedee, no fishermen [except in ch. 21, which is disregarded as not having been a part of the original Gospel], no institution of the Lord's Supper, no marvels at the death of Jesus, no gradual revelation of Jesus, . . . no earthly life of humiliation, no tribute to John the Baptist by anyone, . . . no accusation against Jesus by his family, . . . no healing of a leper, no stilling of a storm at sea, . . . no transfiguration, no kiss by Judas or thirty pieces of silver, no mission of the twelve or the seventy, no beatitudes, no Lord's prayer, . . . no agony in Gethsemane, . . . no fasting, no temptation of Jesus.[2]

These are all instances of omission. Among some of the new features of the Gospel are the wedding feast in Cana, the cripple at the pool of Bethesda, the healing of the man born blind, the raising of Lazarus, and the washing of the disciples' feet. But far more important than such items are certain more pervasive characteristics of the Gospel. Jerusalem and Judea are much more important in Jesus' ministry than one would gather from the Synop-

[1] "Comments on the Fourth Gospel," *Anglican Theological Review,* XII (1929-30), 230. Used by permission.
[2] *John Defends the Gospel* (Chicago: Willett, Clark & Co., 1936), pp. 11f. Used by permission.

tists; his career is longer, running to three years, whereas the Synoptic accounts suggest a shorter period; Jesus' teaching is concerned largely with himself and his own significance rather than with the Kingdom of God and the ethical will of God; and the style of the teaching is quite different: instead of short, epigrammatic utterances we have long, involved, rather repetitious discourses, and instead of simple parables we have elaborate allegories. Still further differences are referred to in Dr. Garvie's essay.

Since it is clear that the author of this Gospel was acquainted with Mark, at least, among the other Gospels, these departures from the Synoptic tradition must point, in part, to peculiarities in the author's purpose. That purpose was undoubtedly many-sided and complex. It was partly concerned with the two interests we have considered earlier: persecution and heresy. It was certainly in part apologetic—that is, the book was aimed at interpreting Christianity in terms acceptable to certain Greek minds and at answering certain objections to Christianity which were prevalent in the pagan society in which the author lived. As Colwell points out, Christianity was often accused of being an obscure Jewish movement, or a proletarian, if not revolutionary, movement, or a superstition. John by his selection of material sought to show that these charges were false. Christians also found themselves in frequent controversy with Jews; John sought to provide data from the life and words of Jesus for use in these controversies. As we read the Gospel we shall see many instances of this apologetic interest.

But the profounder purpose of the author was to present the inner, spiritual meaning of Jesus' life and words. He felt that Mark—as well as Matthew and Luke, if he knew these Gospels—was inadequate. Many of the facts, to be sure, were stated in that Gospel or in those Gospels; but the essential meaning of the facts was not brought out. That meaning John sought to set forth; he did so with great boldness and in a way to which, as I have said, Christian devotion has responded throughout the centuries.

24

Thus we see that the purpose of the writer was not historical in the ordinary sense. This is not to say that the book is altogether unhistorical, but rather that—if by "history" we mean the external facts, mere incidents in Jesus' career or his literal words—the author is not interested in being historical. It is what Christ *really* meant that he is trying to present, and this meaning only the Spirit can reveal. The book is thus more drama than history, and we must read it as such if we would understand both what it has to say and also the significance of the differences between it and the earlier Gospels.

The Gospel can be outlined in various ways. With the publishers' permission, I give below the analysis of the Gospel which appears in one of the best of recent commentaries, that of G. H. C. Macgregor. This book, along with those of Ernest C. Colwell and R. H. Strachan already referred to, deserves a place beside the books mentioned on p. 1066 of *ABC*. The reader of the Gospel and of the following pages will do well to refer back constantly to the outline. It will enable him to keep his bearings as he proceeds slowly through the Gospel.

PRELUDE. CHAPTER 1

1. Prologue: The Incarnation of the Logos. (1-18.)
2. Historical Introduction: The Old Master and the New. (19-51.)

ACT I. THE NEW GOSPEL AND THE OLD

1. The Relation of the New to the Old.
   Illustrations:
   (i) Water turned into Wine. (2:1-11.)
   (ii) Cleansing of the Temple. (2:12-22.)
   Themes:
   (i) The New Birth—in relation to Pharisaism. (2:23–3:13; 3:31-36.)
   (ii) The New Master—in relation to the Baptist. (3:22-30.)
   (iii) The New Worship—in relation to the Samaritans. (4:1-42.)

2. The Appropriation of the New Gospel.
> Illustrations:
>> (i) The Officer's Son healed: Christ restores Life. (4:43-54.)
>> (ii) The 5,000 fed: Christ sustains Life. (6:1-15.)
>> (iii) Christ walks on the Water: The ever-present Saviour. (6:16-21.)
> Theme:
>> The partaking of Christ the Bread of Life. (6:22-71.)

3. The Result of the New Gospel.
> Illustration:
>> The Lame Man healed on the Sabbath. (5:1-16.)
> Theme:
>> Religion not restraint but Life. (5:17-47; 7:15-24; 8:12-20.)

ACT II. THE CONFLICT OF THE NEW GOSPEL WITH THE OLD

1. The Divine Origin of the Christ.
> Illustration:
>> Jesus and his Brothers. (7:1-14, 25-27.)
> Theme:
>> Christ's Divine Commission. (7:28–8:11; 8:21-59.)

2. The Divine Nature of the Christ.
> Illustration:
>> The Blind Man healed. (9:1-38.)
> Theme:
>> Christ the Light, the Good Shepherd, the Door. (9:39–10:42.)

3. The Divine Work of the Christ—the Gift of Life and the Awaking of Faith.
> Illustration:
>> The Raising of Lazarus. (11:1-57.)
> Themes:
>> (i) The Homage of a Disciple. (12:1-8.)
>> (ii) The Homage of the Jews. (12:9-19.)
>> (iii) The Homage of the Gentile World. (12:20-36.)
> Conclusion:
>> The Struggle of Faith with Unbelief. (12:37-50.)

THE GOSPEL OF JOHN

ACT III. THE ENJOYMENT OF THE NEW GOSPEL: CHRIST'S COMMUNION WITH HIS OWN

Illustrations:
  (i) The Washing of the Disciples' Feet. (13:1-38.)
  (ii) The Allegory of the Vine. (15:1-17.)

Themes:
  (i) The Time of Separation. (15:18–16:33.)
  (ii) The Promised Communion. (14:1-31.)
  (iii) The Prayer of Consecration. (17:1-26.)

FINALE

1. The Arrest and Trial. (18:1–19:16.)
2. The Crucifixion of Christ. (19:17-42.)
3. The Resurrection of Christ. (20:1-31.)

EPILOGUE

The Appendix. (21:1-25.) [3]

The reader will notice that in this outline of Macgregor the materials of the Gospel often appear out of order. This it is because Macgregor, along with many other students of the fourth Gospel, is convinced that the document of this Gospel at a very early stage in its history suffered some accident which dislocated parts of its text—in some such way as the pages of a letter often get mixed. Macgregor's reconstruction, which for the most part agrees with the Moffatt translation of the N.T., attempts to restore the Gospel's original form.

One must acknowledge that a more logical arrangement can be secured in this way. But, after all, who knows that the original Gospel was as "logical" as we might think it ought to be? In the following pages I have taken what seemed the safer course: the readings are presented in the traditional order, but usually attention is called to points where there is serious question of correct placement. The reader may form his own opinion.

[3] G. H. C. Macgregor, *The Gospel of John* (New York and London: Harper & Bros., [1928], pp. 1f. Used by permission.

THE FOURTH GOSPEL AND THE LATER EPISTLES

Reading 1: John 1:1-5

THE WORD OF GOD

1. Notice that this Gospel, like the Gospel of Luke, begins with a brief introductory explanation (cf. Lk. 1:1-4 and Jn. 1:1-18). It is customary to speak of the "Preface" of Luke's Gospel and the "Prologue" of John's. What seems to be the general purpose of each of these introductions? What are some of the striking differences between them?

2. Turn to Gen. 1:1 and note that this Gospel begins in the same way as the account of creation. Observe also in this connection Heb. 11:3.

3. Read *ABC*, pp. 1066*b*-67*a*, and formulate in your notebook as carefully as you can the meaning of "the Word."

We have already noted the fact that the author of this Gospel, whom I shall call "John" in spite of the uncertainties of authorship, is interested not so much in the bare words and deeds of Jesus' earthly career as in what he has found to be the spiritual meaning of those words and deeds. This general character of the Gospel has been sufficiently discussed in the preceding pages. Now observe that before presenting the several events of Jesus' earthly life which seem to him most significant, John sets forth in a kind of frontispiece to his book his understanding of who and what Jesus really was. To say that Jesus was a man, born at such and such a time and place, is to say what is true enough, this writer would have agreed, but not the really important truth. To find that truth, he tells us, we must go back to the "beginning," when God created the heavens and the earth. For Christ was nothing less than the divine Agent through whom this creation was accomplished.

The conception that God created the world through an Agent or Mediator was a common one among both Greeks and Jews in John's day. The conception has a complicated origin and history, which we cannot trace here. (*ABC*, as you have seen, throws a good deal of light on the matter.)

28

According to Gen. 1, God created the world by simply speaking (v. 3) : "And God said, Let there be, . . . and there was . . ."; or, as the Epistle to the Hebrews says (11:3) : "The worlds have been framed by the word of God." But not only was the word of God the only instrument of creation, it was also the medium of God's revelation of himself to men. Recall how often in the Prophets we are told that "the word of the Lord" came to Amos, Jeremiah, or Ezekiel.

Now in the course of several centuries this "word" had in ways strange to us, come to be more and more distinguished from God himself until for many in John's time it had come to be thought of almost as a separate Being. One reason for this development was that many thinkers, both Greek and Jewish, had come to feel that God himself was so holy or so infinitely transcendent that it was impossible to think of him as having direct contact with this world and its life. He needed a Mediator; that Mediator was the Logos, the Word. The Word, then (*logos* was one of the Greek terms for "word") , was the creative and revealing activity of God, a part of God and yet distinguished from him. The Word was that *through* which God made the world and reveals himself to finite men.

Now John finds, as we shall see in the next *Reading*, the clue to the real meaning of Jesus in this conception of the creative and revealing Word.

Reading 2: John 1:6-18
THE WORD MADE FLESH

1. Notice that the writer interrupts the high argument about the Word to say something about John the Baptist. Does this not seem like a digression? Would you gather that the author is more interested in what John the Baptist *was* or in what he was *not?* Why does the author think it important to make this digression? Read *ABC*, p. 1067a.

2. Notice that the three parts of v. 14 (without the parenthesis) answer exactly to the three clauses of v. 1.

3. Consider the emphatic statement "The Word became

29

flesh" (v. 14) in the light of what was said earlier about Docetism (see above, p. 19).

It has been observed by many (this was first called to my attention by a sermon of G. Campbell Morgan's years ago) that vv. 1 and 14 are the key verses in this Prologue. In v. 1 we have such a statement as John thinks a contemporary philosopher might make; in v. 14 we have his own statement as a Christian.

"In the beginning was the Word," says the Philosopher.
"Yes, *and the Word became flesh,"* says the Christian.
"The Word was with God," says the Philosopher.
"Yes, but it also *dwelt among us,"* says the Christian.
"The Word was GOD," says the Philosopher.
"Yes, *full of grace and truth,"* says the Christian.

And if v. 18 is included, the conversation can be taken one step further. *"No man hath seen God at any time,"* says the Philosopher.

"That is true," says the Christian, "but *the only begotten Son, who is in the bosom of the Father, he hath declared him."*

For, as John saw things, Jesus Christ was the incarnation of the Word. The Logos was not a merely impersonal being but a personal reality. He was God's own Son; indeed, he was the very One whom (as the First Epistle of John says) "our hands handled" (v. 1). That opening verse of the Epistle, so reminiscent of this opening section of the Gospel, is worth quoting entire in this connection: "That which was from the beginning, that which we have heard, that which we have seen with our eyes, that which we beheld, and our hands handled, concerning the Word of life."

John has pointed out (vv. 4-5) that the Word of God, both creative and revealing, was in the world all the time, but men had not been able to see the light of its revelation nor to receive the divine life it was able to impart. But now in Christ the light has been made clear, and the life is made available for all who will believe on him. Even so, Christ's own people have, by and large, not received him; but those who have received him have been reborn to become the very sons of God, and God has himself become known to them as grace and truth.

Vv. 1 and 14 together make an unusually good text for a sermon on Christ as the revelation of God, as does v. 18 also. V. 12 is another good text. Observe also that most of the notes to be emphasized later in the Gospel are struck in the Prologue: Jesus' superiority to John, Jesus' rejection by the Jewish nation, Jesus as the Son and the Revealer of God, the new birth from above.

Reading 3: John 1:19-34
JESUS AND JOHN THE BAPTIST

1. It is interesting to note that John, like Mark, gives us no details about Jesus' birth or early life. Why does he not do so? Would you say that the same reason, or reasons, apply in the case of Mark?

2. Using a concordance, note the references to John the Baptist in the Gospels. Is there not a sermon on John in these passages?

3. Read *ABC,* p. 1067*b*f.

John begins his Gospel proper, as Mark does also, with the preaching of John the Baptist. But notice the differences. In Mark, the Baptist is introduced not only as the forerunner but also as the baptizer of Jesus; in John, he is brought in only as a witness to Jesus, who is "the Lamb of God, that taketh away the sin of the world" (v. 29) and the one who "baptizeth with the Holy Spirit" (v. 33). There is no suggestion in the fourth Gospel that Jesus himself was baptized.

In connection with this omission it is well to remember that the believers in John the Baptist in the period when this Gospel was written (there were organized followers of the Baptist for more than a century after his death) would almost certainly have appealed to the fact that Jesus was baptized by John as an argument for John's superiority to Jesus. Would the greater, they would have asked, have been baptized by the lesser? Matthew introduces into his story of Jesus' baptism an explanation of how and why this happened (see Mt. 3:13f.); but John simply omits any reference to the baptism.

Observe also that John the Baptist is represented as affirming in clear words that he is not the Christ. His followers in the time of the fourth Gospel, about the end of the first century or later, were probably claiming that he was. These false claims on John the Baptist's behalf perhaps account for the fact that the fourth Gospel has little, if anything, to say by way of tribute to John. In the Synoptic Gospels the Baptist appears as a man of heroic stature. Jesus bestows on him the highest praise, and the whole account of him is such as to let us see how amply that praise was deserved. But in the fourth Gospel, nothing is said to the Baptists' credit, unless some praise is intended for his humility. Certainly, whether intended or not, *we* can find a lesson here: he took no credit to himself and made no claim for himself. He sought to lose himself in the service of the "one greater." He was glad when some of his disciples left him to follow Jesus. Such readiness to efface oneself for the sake of another or a cause is as exemplary as it is rare.

Reading 4: John 1:35-51
JESUS' FIRST DISCIPLES

1. Read Mk. 1:16-20, Mt. 4:18-22, and Lk. 5:1-11, and notice similarities and divergences when compared with this passage in John.

2. It is striking that both John and Mark identify Jesus as coming from Nazareth and make no mention of his Bethlehem origin. Can you think of a possible reason for this?

3. With a concordance discover what reference, if any, is made to Andrew, Philip, and Nathanael in the other Gospels.

4. Is there not a sermon in "Come and see" (v. 46)?

Here is John's account of how Jesus' first disciples came to be associated with him. They had been with the Baptist, but when the latter pointed out Jesus to them, they left their former leader and set out after Jesus. Jesus invited them to spend the day with him, and they were never afterward able to leave him.

It was John the Baptist, then, who introduced Andrew and an unnamed disciple to Jesus. Soon afterward Andrew brought his brother, Simon Peter. The next day Jesus went out of Judea into Galilee, and Philip became his disciple. But Philip had presumably heard of Jesus from Andrew and Peter, for he was from the same town, Bethsaida. Not long afterward Philip found Nathanael. It is interesting to note that all five of these men became disciples of Jesus because of the personal influence of others. So it has always been. The early church spread largely through the personal witnessing of believers; and the church still grows chiefly in that way.

And what did it mean to be a "disciple" of Jesus? The word meant what we mean by "pupil," and much more, for a disciple was a pupil who lived with his teacher that he might share not only his master's thought but also his master's life through friendship. The disciples of Jesus, then, were his pupils, his friends, his companions. In what sense can we be his disciples still?

Observe the titles used in this section in referring to Jesus. There are a surprising number, suggesting the scope and the richness of the meaning of Jesus for those who believed on him: "Lamb of God," "Rabbi," "Messiah," "Son of God," "King of Israel," "Son of Man." In the other Gospels such acknowledgments of Jesus' messiahship come only toward the end of his career. John is ascribing to these first disciples at the beginning of their association with Jesus beliefs about him which they came to hold only after long association with him, indeed in some cases only after his death and resurrection. Be sure to read in connection with this passage *ABC,* p. 1068*b.*

Reading 5: John 2:1-12

THE CHANGING OF THE WATER INTO WINE

1. Notice in *ABC,* pp. 1068-69, the several ways in which this passage has been interpreted.

2. The last sentence in v. 11 tells us that Jesus by this miracle "manifested his glory." This note is largely lacking in the Synoptic Gospels, where Jesus is represented, as often as not, as trying to conceal his miracles. Can you suggest a reason for this difference?

This passage well exemplifies the difficulties of taking this Gospel as literally historical in the same way we take the earlier Gospels. This story of the changing of the water into wine is hard to accept as the record of an actual incident, not so much because of its miraculous character as because the occasion of the miracle seems so trivial. This story does not appear in the Synoptics. As *ABC* suggests, the passage has sometimes been taken as an allegory. There is no indication that the writer intended it only as such— he doubtless believed the incident actually occurred just as he records it. At the same time, it must be recognized that he finds a spiritual meaning in the story and that he records the incident not for its own sake but for the sake of that spiritual meaning. This meaning may well have been that Jesus transformed the "water of Judaism" into the "wine of Christianity."

Preachers have often used this text for sermons on the power of Christ to transform life. This involves an allegorical use of Scripture, which is always dangerous, since one is likely to be merely reading one's own ideas into the Bible text. Still, it may well be that something like this was in the author's mind; and if this is an allegory, the true way to interpret it is allegorically. What one must be on guard against is giving an allegorical interpretation to a text which was meant quite simply and literally.

Perhaps the passage provides a sounder basis for a sermon on Jesus' friendliness and geniality—his willingness to attend and to promote the pleasure of the wedding feast (cf. Mt. 11:18f.) —although it must be added that this was certainly not the point the writer was interested in making.

Reading 6: John 2:13-25

THE CLEANSING OF THE TEMPLE

1. Recall the Synoptic accounts of this act of Jesus and compare them with this one. What differences do you notice?

2. Read *ABC*, p. 1069, for alternative ways of explaining the different order which this incident has in John.

3. The animals and pigeons were on sale for the sacrifices. Does Jesus object to the selling itself in the outer court of the Temple, or is his objection to something dishonest in the way it was done? See *ABC*, pp. 900*a* and 986*a*, for two different possible answers to this question.

One of the most striking divergences of John from the Synoptic account of Jesus' career consists in his references to several visits of Jesus to Jerusalem and Judea. According to Mark, Matthew, and Luke, Jesus' ministry lay in Galilee till the final weeks of his life, when he went down to Jerusalem to celebrate the Passover, as Jews from all over Palestine—and, indeed, from all over the world—were accustomed to do as often as possible. But John tells of several visits to Jerusalem, and much of the important action of the Gospel takes place in Judea. It is these visits in John's Gospel which make the teaching career of Jesus, as he records it, extend to two or three years, whereas in the Synoptic Gospels one would gather that it lasted only for one year or less. Here we have the first of these visits.

The cleansing of the Temple in the Synoptic Gospels is placed at the beginning of Passion Week; and it probably belongs there. We have seen that John does not hesitate to alter the historical order if he can thus better set forth what seems to him the true meaning of Jesus' life. No doubt this is such a case. Just as faith in Jesus as the Christ is represented as existing from the very start, so also hostility toward him as the Christ develops almost at once.

Observe that it is "the Jews" who are hostile—not *some* of the Jews, or a particular party of Jews, like the Pharisees. This, we shall find, is characteristic of this Gospel. Its author sees all the Jews as hostile to Christ—which means that almost certainly he was not a Jew himself and that he quite certainly was not appealing to Jewish readers. Would one gather from reading this passage about Jesus' conversation with "the Jews" that Jesus himself was a Jew? What does this mean as to the probable attitude of this author toward Jews? We shall have frequent occasion to return to this theme during the reading of this Gospel.

The story of the cleansing of the Temple shows us one of the genuine aspects of Jesus' character which not infrequently appears in the Gospels, though rarely so clearly —his capacity for indignation and forceful action when confronted by some grievous wrong. Note, however, that the "scourge of cords" is mentioned only in this Gospel. The other Gospels simply say he "cast them out."

Reading 7: John 3:1-13

THE BIRTH FROM ABOVE

1. Is Nicodemus mentioned outside of the fourth Gospel? Some have found a correspondence between this story in John and the Synoptic account of the rich young ruler (see Mk. 10:17f. and parallels in Matthew and Luke). Do you see any signs of this correspondence?

2. In this passage occurs the only reference in the fourth Gospel to the kingdom of God, which appears so constantly in the Synoptic accounts of Jesus' teaching. What conception takes its place in this Gospel? Read *ABC,* p. 1070*a*.

3. Could v. 13 have been actually spoken by Jesus? Why?

4. Would you say that Nicodemus was a sincere seeker after truth, or merely curious, or contemptuous, or hostile?

Jesus' disciples were generally men of very humble circumstances, although it is notable that we do not learn this from this Gospel. John has little, if anything, to say about the poor and does not speak of Jesus' associating with humble people, as the Synoptics do. Nicodemus was a leading man among the Pharisees. He visited Jesus by night. Opinions will always differ as to whether the author is meaning to suggest cowardice and stealth on Nicodemus' part or whether he is merely recording a casual detail of the record.

Nicodemus opens the conversation with a reference to Jesus' miracles as proving him to be a "teacher come from God." Macgregor points out that Jesus answers not so much these words as the question "What must I do to have life?" which, according to the Synoptics, the rich young ruler asked, and which Jesus apparently regards as the real question in the mind of Nicodemus. In Mark (10:21), Jesus gives an *ethical* answer to this question: "Sell whatsoever thou hast, and give to the poor, and thou shalt have treasure in heaven: and come, follow me." In John, he gives a mystical, or "spiritual," answer: "You must . . . be born from above" (Moffatt). Here is a note nowhere struck in the Synoptic Gospels, but everywhere present in Paul, who describes the believer as a "new creation," as well as in this Gospel which, as we saw in the Prologue, thinks of Christ as having brought new life as well as new light.

This new life is a gift of the Spirit, although baptism is apparently mentioned as the seal of it. This must be what is meant by the allusion to birth "of water and the Spirit" (Jn. 3:5). V. 8 involves a play on words. The Greek word for "wind" is also the word for "spirit." Just as we cannot deny the reality of the wind, though we cannot understand it, so we cannot deny the reality of the Spirit and its workings, mysterious as they are.

Reading 8: John 3:14-21

SALVATION AND JUDGMENT

1. Read Num. 21:8-9. The author of the fourth Gospel, together with other ancient allegorical interpreters of the

O.T., saw in this passage a reference to the crucifixion. Do you think it is at all likely that the original writer had anything like that in his mind?

2. Notice that this writer regards the crucifixion of Jesus as a part of his exaltation. In being lifted up on a piece of wood (like the serpent in the wilderness) he was also lifted to God. Only by way of his death could he return to his Father. Do you recall anything like this way of interpreting the death of Jesus in Paul or the Synoptics? (See *Reading* 30.)

3. Notice how the terms "light" and "life," key words in the Prologue, occur and recur in this passage.

4. We have seen that the idea of the kingdom of God, so prevalent in the Synoptics, is replaced almost entirely in this Gospel with the concept of "life," or "eternal life." In this passage the idea of judgment is introduced. How does the understanding of the judgment in this Gospel differ from that in the Synoptics?

One of the interesting features of John's Gospel is the way a report of the words of Jesus gradually turns into a discourse by the Evangelist himself. In Jn. 3:1-21 we have an excellent example of this. The passage begins as an account of a conversation between Jesus and Nicodemus, but by the time we reach v. 13 it is clearly John himself who is speaking, for the final ascension of Jesus is mentioned as having already occurred. This feature of the Gospel is obviously in line with what we have observed to be its character: it is an interpretation of the *significance* of Jesus, not a bare, factual account of his acts and words. In these, merely as such, this author is comparatively uninterested. He is a preacher rather than a historian. And it will help us to understand the true character and message of John's Gospel if we think of it as a series of dramatic sermons based on his understanding of the words and acts of Jesus.

The significance of Jesus, as it is brought out here, consists primarily in his being the revelation of God: he is the "light." The writer sees the world generally as "sitting in darkness" and in death—the darkness of ignorance of God and the death of separation from him. To save men, God sends his only Son to impart the knowledge of himself and, therefore, both light and life. This knowledge of God, which *is* itself eternal life, is not merely a future attainment; it may be a present experience. Likewise, judgment (v. 19—this word may be better rendered "condemnation") does not wait till the end of the world, but is even now present whenever one rejects the light.

Christ did not come to condemn us, but to save us; but when we do not "believe"—that is, when we reject him as the revelation of God—we condemn ourselves: "We are judged already."

It is important to observe that, as this writer sees it, the quality of our conduct has a direct and important bearing upon our capacity for seeing the truth (cf. vv. 20-21; 7:17).

Written Work.—Write a full outline of a sermon on Jn. 3:16, bringing out as many as possible of the characteristic Johannine ideas which your reading of these three chapters has disclosed.

Reading 9: John 3:22-36
THE BAPTIST'S SECOND WITNESS

1. Compare Jn. 3:23 with Mk. 1:14, noting another divergence between the Johannine and the Synoptic accounts of Jesus' career.

2. Do you see any way of harmonizing the clear, unhesitating witness of John to Jesus in this passage with Lk. 7:18f.?

3. This passage contains another instance of the report of a speech by another becoming a discourse of the Evangelist himself. In v. 27 John the Baptist is speaking, and in v. 36 the Evangelist is speaking. At what point, would you say, does the transition occur?

4. Many scholars believe that vv. 22-30 have been displaced and that they originally followed 2:11. Do you see the reasons for this view? Macgregor places them after 3:36.

This account of an overlapping between John's ministry and that of Jesus marks a departure from the Synoptic tradition. John the Baptist, when confronted with the fact that Jesus' following was growing more rapidly than his, repeats what he has said in an earlier passage. He rejoices in Jesus' success, declaring that he is only the bridegroom's friend (we would say the "best man") ; Jesus is the bridegroom, to whom the honor belongs.

Vv. 31-36 emphasize a note struck over and over again in this Gospel, namely, that Jesus "was sent" from heaven or that he "comes" from God. This was a frequent way of referring to the Messiah and John's favorite way of referring to Christ.

The writer of this Gospel, as we have already seen, never uses the word "faith," but he does talk constantly of "believing on Christ," as we have already seen and now see again. "Believing on Christ" apparently means accepting him as the Son of God and as the revelation of the Father. Note the difference between this understanding and Paul's way of thinking of "faith." With Paul faith is a matter of reliance upon the mercy of God offered in Christ. The two conceptions do not contradict each other, but there is a difference of emphasis.

Reading 10: John 4:1-25
THE SAMARITAN WOMAN

1. Observe on a map of Palestine (there is one in *ABC*) where Samaria lies with respect to Galilee and Judea. Why did Jews often prefer the roundabout way through Perea, which lay east of the Jordan, when journeying from Judea to Galilee?

2. Read *ABC* on this passage, pp. 1070*b*f. See if you can find 'Askar on the map. Jacob's Well is about one half mile south of this place.

Jesus' life was lived almost entirely among Jews, whether in Galilee or Judea. The Christian movement, however, spread largely among Gentiles. Even as early as 50 A.D. it was clear that the Jewish nation, by and large, had rejected the claims of Christ. Chs. 9-11 of Paul's letter to the Romans place this fact beyond any doubt. When the fourth Gospel was written, a half century or so later, we can be sure that very few men and women of Jewish birth belonged to the church. John is addressing himself entirely to Gentile readers. This being true, it is natural that he should gladly avail himself of the opportunity of recounting an experience Jesus had in what was, strictly speaking, a non-Jewish country—Samaria—and of telling of the cordial way in which he was received there. Jesus' success in Samaria on this occasion becomes to John a sign of the success the gospel of Christ was to have in the non-Jewish world (Macgregor).

The story itself is clear enough. Jesus, tired from walking, is resting at noon on the ground near Jacob's Well, when a Samaritan woman comes to draw some water. Jesus asks her for a drink, and when she expresses surprise that he should address her—a woman and a Samaritan— Jesus goes on to speak to her of the "water springing up unto eternal life" (4:14b). Here we have the Evangelist again interpreting Christ as the giver of life, this time using the symbol of a spring of living water.

There follows a brief discussion of the woman's past life, of which Jesus reveals a miraculous knowledge, and of the differences of opinion between Jews and Samaritans as to where one should worship. Jesus is represented as announcing that the time has come when the true worship of God can be carried out neither in the mountain nor in Jerusalem, but wherever true worshipers (that is, the Christians) worship, in Spirit and in truth.

The passage concludes with Jesus' dramatic statement that he is the Messiah. According to the Synoptics, Jesus makes no such avowal till near the close of his life. Which account seems to you more plausible on this point?

Reading 11: John 4:26-42
SUCCESS IN SAMARIA

1. Why are the disciples surprised when they find Jesus engaged in this conversation? Suggest two reasons. What does this little touch in the story tell us of the difference Christ has made in subsequent centuries?

2. Compare Jn. 4:35-38 with Mt. 9:37-38.

The return of the disciples interrupts the conversation; so we do not hear just what effect Jesus' announcement of his Messiahship has on the woman. She leaves her pitcher in her haste to tell her friends in the town about this strange man who has told her everything she has done (an understandable exaggeration).

Large numbers of the townspeople come out to see Jesus. Moved by his conversation with the woman and with this fruit of it, Jesus has forgotten his hunger (and presumably his thirst) and tells his disciples, who urge him to eat, that he has food they do not know about.

He goes on to explain that the fields are ripe for harvest even though he has only just now sown the seed (Macgregor). Only a few hours ago, or less, he was speaking for the first time to the unknown woman; and now all these Samaritans have come to believe on him. The writer of the Gospel sees in this incident a sign of the readiness of the Gentiles to receive the Christian message.

It is interesting to observe that nothing is said in this whole story about the woman's being a sinner and needing to repent, nor yet of any penitence on her part. Jesus is not said to have forgiven her. This note, so prominent in Synoptic stories of Jesus' dealings with women of this kind, is curiously lacking. We have already seen that John has little to say about the poor; in the same way he says little, if anything, about sinners.

Notice again the power of personal testimony. One woman wins a whole city. Observe also, in v. 42, the writer's emphasis upon the importance of firsthand personal religious experience. This is a good text for a sermon.

Reading 12: John 4:43-54

THE HEALING OF THE OFFICIAL'S SON

Do not vv. 43 f. suggest that this writer thinks of Judea as being Jesus' real home (as would have seemed appropriate for the Messiah) even though, as we have seen, he knows that Jesus grew up in Nazareth of Galilee? Read *ABC,* p. 1071*b,* on this.

2. Read Mt. 8:5-13 and Lk. 7:1-10. Notice the similarities and differences between this story, told by the two Synoptists, and the story we are now examining from John. Would you say that two distinct incidents are being reported, or is it more likely that we have here two accounts of the same miracle?

3. In what two senses is the word "believe" used in vv. 50 and 53?

There is some reason for thinking that a new section of the Gospel begins with this incident (see above, page 26). Observe that the incident occurs in Cana, where Jesus performed his first miracle. Read again the story of the changing of the water into wine (2:1-11). Macgregor points out further correspondences between the two stories (p. 123): "In both narratives Jesus replies to a request for help with apparent harshness, the petitioner continues to trust, and finally Jesus grants the request with unexpected fulness."

The initial apparent harshness is designed to test the faith of the one who has made the request in each case. Prayer must be importunate and faith persistent if either is to be effectual. But if these conditions *are* fulfilled, God will grant us "even more than we ask." This is a lesson frequently and more explicitly taught in the Synoptic Gospels and in the Epistles.

The word (v 46*b*) rendered "nobleman" is better translated "king's official" (Goodspeed) —that is, an officer of the government. John almost certainly thought of him as a non-Jew. Thus the story accentuates the point made in the

43

preceding section: the new revelation, rejected by the Jews, is received by the Gentiles.

Reading 13: John 5:1-17
JESUS AND THE SABBATH LAW

1. Many scholars believe that a dislocation of material has occurred at this point and that originally ch. 6 preceded ch. 5. Notice how the two chapters begin and see, if you can, the reason for this view.

2. Notice what *ABC*, p. 1072*a*, says as to the identity of the "feast," or festival, referred to. The Passover was held in April and Pentecost in May. Other possibilities are Purim in March, Tabernacles in October, and Dedication in December.

3. In connection with v. 10, read Num. 15:32f.; Neh. 13:15; and Jer. 17:21. Did Jesus' critics not have good *legal* basis for their protests?

We have already observed many times that this author is very much concerned to make clear the supreme importance and worth of Christianity as compared with all other religious movements. Jesus' superiority to John is mentioned often. The changing of the water into wine was, as we have seen, probably a symbolic representation of the superiority of Christianity to Judaism. The same idea appears in Jesus' conversation with Nicodemus and in the story of the Samaritan woman. Now, in the present *Reading*, Jesus' authority over the Jewish Law is affirmed and illustrated.

The fact that in Christ the old Law is superseded, if not invalidated entirely, was suggested in the Prologue to this Gospel: "The law was given through Moses; grace and truth through Jesus Christ" (1:17). But now an actual example is given of Jesus' independence of the Law. He heals a lame man on the Sabbath, telling him to take up his mat (a more accurate translation than "bed") and to walk around.

The Synoptic Gospels confirm the statement of this

44

writer that Jesus' freedom in the use of the Sabbath was one of the most important sources of hostility toward him.

Notice again that the writer rarely differentiates (as the Synoptists do) between various parties of Jews. He speaks simply of "the Jews," as though all Jews were hostile—indeed, as though Jesus and his disciples were not also Jews! Can we avoid seeing signs of anti-Semitism in this writer? More will be said on this point later. Meantime, do we not have here a reminder that the gospel of Christ comes to us through channels that are not always perfectly clear of human weakness and sin?

Reading 14: John 5:18-30
THE FATHER AND THE SON

1. Observe that, except for vv. 24 and 30, this whole section is written in the third person. Is it not clear that we have here, as *ABC* suggests (p. 1072*b*), a theological exposition by the writer rather than the words of Jesus himself? The words in such passages are placed in Jesus' mouth in the way a dramatist puts discourses in the mouths of his characters. A comparison of the style of such discourses as this with that of such a passage as Mt. 5–7, or Lk. 15, will make the point clear.

2. Note the statement of *ABC* that this is the only passage in any of the Gospels where a resurrection to damnation as well as a resurrection to life is spoken of. Paul, along with the Synoptics, says nothing of a resurrection of those who are not "in Christ." The resurrection of both righteous and unrighteous is referred to, however, in Dan. 12:2 and in Acts 24:15. Look up these passages.

In this passage, as in parts of the Prologue, we have an interpretation of the relation of Christ to God as this Christian teacher at the end of the first century sees it. The exposition takes its start from Jesus' answer to those who had objected to his healing on the Sabbath. "My Father is always working [that is, Sabbaths and all], and I also must not stop doing good" (Jn. 4:17). Then, we are

45

told, "the Jews" hated him the more because he made himself equal with God by calling God (in a special sense) his Father.

This remark leads the author into his discussion of the relation of Christ to God. He mentions, first, the intimate knowledge of the Father which the Son enjoys (this is near to the idea, so frequently found in this Gospel, of Christ as the revelation of God, the "light"); then Christ's power of imparting new life (also often emphasized) is affirmed, as well as his being God's agent for the judging of the world. Notice that both the life and the judgment are not merely future; they are present realities. The believer has already "passed out of death into life" (5:24), just as those who believe not are condemned already (see 3:18). In v. 25, John is obviously speaking of the *spiritually* dead as being raised through Christ even now, whereas in v. 28, he is apparently referring to the events which, it was believed, would occur at the end of the world.

Observe how near v. 24 is to Paul's teaching in Rom. 8:1f.

Written Work.—Outline fully a sermon on Jn. 5:24, emphasizing "listening," "believing," and "life" ("life" as over against both "condemnation" and "death").

Reading 15: John 5:31-47
TESTIMONY TO CHRIST

1. Notice still another reference to John the Baptist as a witness to Christ.

2. Observe that in v. 39 "search" in the A.V. becomes "you search" in later versions and translations. Which rendering (the Greek word may be either imperative or indicative) makes better sense?

3. Read carefully *ABC* on this passage, p. 1073*a*.

This discourse, which our writer dramatically places on the lips of Jesus, began, it will be remembered, in a controversy over Jesus' disregard of the Sabbath (see the preceding *Reading*). Now the polemical character of the discourse becomes more conspicuous. Jesus is defending his authority as the Christ against Jewish denials of it. He calls to witness not only John but also the work which he himself is carrying out. Indeed, God himself is a witness for Jesus as the Messiah. And only their dullness of mind and heart keeps "the Jews" from hearing this divine testimony. *ABC* suggests that "the Ephesian environment" of the writer "has colored the record" here; this means, in other words, that the struggle between the church and the synagogue in such a city as Ephesus, at the end of the first century when this book was written (see above, p. 16), is reflected to some extent in these words ascribed to Jesus. Can one doubt that this is true, in view of what we have discovered about the purpose and method of this writer?

V. 39 provides a good text for a sermon on why we should search the Scriptures. We should do so because Christ is to be found there. "Eternal life" cannot be found in the mere words of Scripture. Jesus' critics have been searching the words of Scripture, thinking that life was to be found there; but they were mistaken, Jesus says. Life can be found only in Christ, and the Scriptures are valuable because they lead us to him.

Reading 16: John 6:1-21

FEEDING THE FIVE THOUSAND

1. This is one of the very few incidents which are reported by all four Gospels. Compare this account with Mt. 14:13-21; Mk. 6:31-44; and Lk. 9:10-17.

2. Can you think of a reason why this writer finds it appropriate to state that the time of Christ's feeding of the multitude was the time of the Passover? Can this have anything to do with the superiority of Christianity to Judaism which this writer is so concerned to maintain?

3. First century writers regularly speak of the "Sea of Galilee," but by the middle of the second century this lake is usually called the "Sea of Tiberias," the name being taken from a town built on its shores in Jesus' own time or

a little later, dedicated to Tiberias the Emperor. Macgregor finds in John's use of both names a hint of the Gospel's date. Does this seem plausible to you?

4. Notice that in the Synoptics the disciples become concerned at the people's hunger at the end of the day, but that in this Gospel Jesus expresses this concern as the people first approach. Which of these descriptions of the occasion seems more likely?

This story, while conforming very closely to the narrative in Mark, is told with a somewhat different purpose than in the Synoptics. There it is presented as an illustration of Jesus' compassion for the multitude of needy people and of his supernatural power. Here, although these notes—or at least the second of them—are not missing, the story is told principally because it serves to set forth the meaning of Jesus as the Bread of Life, as we shall see more clearly in the next reading.

One of the most striking features of the fourth Gospel is its omission of the institution of the Lord's Supper. In a real sense, this feeding of the multitude, as it is interpreted in vv. 35-58, takes its place.

The people, impressed by the miracle, decide that Jesus is the "prophet that should come into the world" (6:14b—A.V.) and want to make him "king." Notice that the word "Messiah," or "Christ," is not used, although both of the expressions used are messianic. This is probably because John uses the term "Christ" in a different sense from that of "prophet" or "king." Jesus *was* the Christ and would have been glad to be acknowledged as such; but he was not a king in the ordinary, or even in a messianic, sense. His kingdom was not of this world.

Reading 17: John 6:22-60
THE BREAD OF LIFE

1. Read *ABC*, p. 1074a (on vv. 26-40), noting signs of the weaving together of two accounts of this discourse of Jesus to form this passage. Notice especially that two different

situations seem to be given for the discourse (vv. 25 and
59) and that there is a great deal of repetition in the passage as it stands.

2. Read the passage through, carefully noting indications that the author is thinking of the meaning of the
sacrament of the Lord's Supper.

All through this Gospel, thus far, we have observed the
emphasis upon life as God's gift through Christ whom "he
hath sent." That was true particularly of the Prologue
and of Jesus' discourses upon the new birth, which he
makes possible, and upon the water of life, which he gives.
Now this same important note is struck again—only this
time bread is the symbol used.

Note how close vv. 32-36 are to paralleling an important
section of the discourse addressed to the woman of Samaria
(Jn. 4:12-14). Jacob corresponds to Moses as the repre-
sentative of Judaism; the water of Jacob's Well answers
to the manna which Moses gave; and, of course, the living
bread which "giveth life unto the world" (6:33b) and
forever ends hunger corresponds with the water "springing
up unto eternal life" (4:14b), after drinking which one
never thirsts again.

This passage is filled with texts for preaching. In what
ways do we think of Christ as the bread of life (v. 35)?
What spiritual hungers does he satisfy? V. 57 is a good
text for a sermon on communion with Christ.

Although, as was noted in the comment on the preceding
Reading, there is no account of the formal institution of
the Lord's Supper in this Gospel, John does include this
long discourse in which the meaning of that sacrament is
unmistakably being set forth. What are we to make of this?
What was John's attitude toward the sacrament? Different
answers are given. Scott answers that his attitude was two-
fold: (1) he recognized "the danger to the higher life of
the Church of an external ordinance, observed as it was
wont to be in a mechanical and superstitious spirit," but
(2) his purpose was not "to disparage the Sacrament, but

to assert the great religious facts in which its real significance consists." (See also *Reading* 32, below.)

Reading 18: John 6:60-71

CRISIS IN GALILEE

1. It has been held that vv. 66-71 are a variant account of the confession of Peter at Caesarea Philippi. Read Mt. 16:13-20 and *ABC*, p. 1075a, and form your own judgment about this view.

2. In v. 64 we are told that Jesus had supernatural knowledge of who should betray him and of who believed on him. Is this consistent with the Synoptic account?

We have already seen that the great multitude, which had followed Jesus across the lake, faded away as Jesus spoke of himself as the "bread of life." Now we are informed that many of his disciples were likewise offended. These "disciples" were not the Twelve, but a larger group, attracted to him but not committed to him as thoroughly as were the Twelve. These were perplexed and offended by Jesus' strange words, and many of them pulled away.

V. 62 is difficult. Is Jesus saying: "You are amazed by what you have heard? That is nothing. Suppose you should see the Son of Man ascending to heaven, where he was before!" Or is he meaning to say: "You find this amazing? But you will better understand the spiritual nature of what I am saying about bread from heaven when the Son of Man shall have returned to the Father" (Macgregor). If the latter is the meaning, v. 63 becomes more intelligible and appropriate.

After these lukewarm followers have left, Jesus turns to the inner circle, the Twelve (v. 67): "Would ye also go away?" Peter answers: "To whom shall we go? thou hast the words of eternal life." The story ends with Jesus' prediction of his betrayal by one of them, whom the author identifies as Judas.

This story exemplifies a rather wide gamut of attitudes

toward Jesus: outright enmity, desertion, betrayal, and faithful discipleship. Here is a possible idea for a sermon.

Reading 19: John 7:1-52
A CONTROVERSY WITH JEWISH CRITICS

1. Many scholars believe the section 7:15-24 is out of place. Whether or not one agrees with this view, it is clear that v. 25 seems to take up the story where v. 14 leaves off. 7:15-24 is regarded as belonging originally after 5:17-47. Do you see the reasons for this? See *ABC* on this point, p. 1075*b*.

2. Read Mk. 3:21f. and contrast the attitude of Jesus' family toward his ministry with that attitude as John understood it. Or do you think Jesus' brothers are here "taunting" him, as *ABC* suggests?

According to the outline we have adopted, this chapter begins the second "act" of this drama. Up to this point the author has been concerned principally with the nature of the gospel of Christ; now for several chapters he presents in various ways the conflict between that gospel and Judaism. This theme has already appeared many times, as we have seen, but now it becomes more dominant and conspicuous.

The phrase "walked in Galilee," near the beginning of the passage, is probably meant, as Macgregor says, to indicate a rather extended stay. Up to this point in John's Gospel one gets the impression that Jesus' "headquarters" were in Judea and that he had come into Galilee only for brief visits. Now John represents him as spending a longer time there. It is the Feast of Tabernacles which provides the occasion for a secret return to Judea. This festival, held in October, commemorated God's care of Israel while the nation was living in tents in the wilderness, and during the eight days of the feast the people lived in tents.

In vv. 25-36, and again in vv. 40-52, the author does what he does very rarely: he distinguishes between various groups of Jesus' contemporaries, finds that some were friendly and some hostile. This approaches the picture in the Synoptic Gospels and is undoubtedly more nearly accurate than the usual lumping together of all "the Jews" as Jesus' enemies.

Notice in vv. 33-36 a feature of this Gospel which we have observed many times before: the emphasis upon the blindness and obtuseness of Jesus' opponents in understanding what he meant by his words.

The author's view that Jesus must go away in order that the Spirit might come is often expressed in this Gospel, as we shall see; and, of course, it corresponds with the actual fact that it was only after the resurrection that the Spirit was given.

V. 42 cannot be taken to mean that John is not familiar with the tradition preserved in Matthew and Luke that Jesus was born in Bethlehem. This verse, however, as well as v. 52, does suggest that this fact about Jesus was not universally known or acknowledged in John's day. John's own position would almost certainly have been that it did not matter where Jesus was born. To him the all-important fact was not that Jesus was the son of David but that he was the Son of God.

Reading 20: John 7:53–8:20
THE SINFUL WOMAN

1. Look up Deut. 22:22 for the Law of Moses to which appeal is made in v. 5.

2. Would you agree with *ABC* (p. 1077*a*) that the woman's sins are not forgiven in 8:11?

The oldest MSS. of the Gospels do not contain the story of the woman taken in adultery. Later MSS. usually contain it, however, sometimes at this point in John and sometimes after Lk. 21:38. It is one of the most striking and appealing stories in the Gospels, and is of undoubtedly ancient origin. There is no reason to deny its authenticity. It may well have belonged to the earliest tradition.

Nothing is more certain, however, than that it did not originally belong to the Gospel of John. Not only is the

MS. evidence against that supposition, but also the style is quite different from that of the Gospel as a whole. Moreover, the subject of the story, the saving of a sinful woman, is one in which the Synoptists, especially Luke, show more interest than does John.

Readers of the story have often speculated upon what Jesus wrote on the ground, or why he wrote at all. (Notice the answers that have been given to this question as they are indicated in *ABC,* p. 1076*b*.) Probably he actually wrote nothing at all; it was a gesture of embarrassment, expressing his pain both at what the woman had done and at what her persecutors were now doing. Macgregor points out that since Jesus was sitting on the ground (v. 2), as Oriental teachers normally did, the "stooping" was not as pronounced as we are accustomed to think. Strachan suggests "hung his head" instead of "stooped down."

The reference to Jesus as "the light of the world" (8:12) takes up one of the notes struck in the Prologue. And the controversy with the Pharisees, which follows this claim of Jesus, again emphasizes their obtuseness in understanding Jesus' spiritual meaning.

Reading 21: John 8:21-59
ANOTHER CONTROVERSY WITH "THE JEWS"

1. Read *ABC* on this passage, pp. 1077f.
2. Compare the controversy of this chapter with that in ch. 6. In both cases, is it not clear that the disputes and issues of a later period, the Gospel writer's period, are being read back into Jesus' own lifetime?

Here is another account of a controversy with "the Jews." This time it is Jesus' origin and authority which are being particularly debated. One notices again, as almost always in this book, the lumping together of all Jews as enemies of Jesus. The author is undoubtedly letting the bitter conflict between church and synagogue in his own period color his understanding of Jesus' own relationships and attitudes. After all, Jesus could hardly have referred to Abraham as *"your* father" (v. 56). And the bitterness of Jesus' words can scarcely be historical. Surely he who said, "Love your enemies," could hardly have spoken some of these ruthless words. Read *ABC,* p. 1078*a,* on this.

Jesus claims to be the preexistent Son of God about whom the author has spoken in the Prologue. This appears in "I am from above" (v. 23), in the phrase "that I am" (vv. 24, 28; cf. Ex. 3:14), in the references to the Father, and in the statement in v. 58: "Before Abraham was born, I am."

One observes again in this passage the author's stress upon the dullness of mind which characterized "the Jews." They insist on taking Jesus' words with crass literalism, although to any ordinary person it would be clear that he is speaking of spiritual realities. For example, Jesus says that the truth will set them free; but they insist that they have never been slaves of any man. Jesus must then try to explain that he means they are the slaves of sin and that this is the slavery from which they will be released if they continue in his words.

Written Work.—Prepare a careful and full outline of a sermon on Jn. 8:31-32. What is meant by "continuing" in Christ's "word"? By "disciples indeed"? What is "the truth" that sets men free? "Free" in what sense?

Reading 22: John 9
THE HEALING OF A MAN BORN BLIND

1. Compare Jesus' teaching in Jn. 9:3 with what he says on the same subject in Lk. 13:1-5.

2 Do you think Jesus would deny any connection between sin and suffering? Consider in this connection Mt. 9:2 and Jn. 5:14.

This very interesting and delightful, as well as illuminating, story falls, as *ABC* indicates (pp. 1078f.), into three parts: the healing itself, the attempts of Jesus' opponents to deny or discount the fact of the healing, and Jesus' final manifestation of himself as the object of faith.

The method of the healing suggests Mk. 7:33 and 8:23, but it is not necessary to suppose that this is only an elaboration of a Synoptic story. As in the case of the healing in Jn. 5, the point of objection on the part of the Pharisees is that Jesus has performed a cure on the Sabbath. They first try to shake the testimony of the healed man; they then seek from his parents a denial that he had been *born* blind, hoping to reduce the significance of the miracle; they finally confront the man with the fact that Jesus had broken the law and therefore could not be from God. The man refuses to get involved in controversies with persons who have more learning and skill in such matters than he; but he takes his stand firmly on the fact: "One thing I know, that, whereas I was blind, now I see" (Jn. 9:25*b*). The story as it proceeds from that point well illustrates our human inclination to hold on to our theories, especially if they serve or support our interests, even in disregard of facts. The Pharisees, when they cannot refute or answer the man, throw him out of the synagogue.

Jesus either happens to meet him later, or seeks him out, and makes himself known as the Christ.

The spiritual lesson of the story is brought out in vv. 39-41.The Pharisees are the really blind; and since their blindness is perverse, they are guilty because of it.

A good sermon can be preached on the story with the central emphasis upon v. 25.

Reading 23: John 10:1-18
THE GOOD SHEPHERD

1. Jot down a few places in the Synoptic Gospels where Jesus uses the figures of the shepherd or the sheepfold.

2. We have an excellent opportunity of observing here the difference between the parable and the allegory. Notice the parable in Lk. 15:4-7. It is the story told to illustrate some one moral or religious truth. In an allegory, each of the items in the story stands for, or symbolizes, some spiritual reality. To which of these categories does this passage belong?

This is one of the most beautiful passages in the fourth Gospel, or in the Bible. Macgregor writes about it (p. 234):

It provides a good example of . . . passages where several short sections, existing perhaps independently in an original source, but dealing with kindred subjects, have been worked up together into a single paragraph. Thus we have here: *first* (1-5), a simple allegory descriptive of the ideal shepherd; *second* (7-10), an interpretation of this in which Christ appears not, as might be expected, as the Shepherd, but as the Door; *third* (11-18), another more natural interpretation in which Jesus himself is pictured as the "Good Shepherd." As a result it is impossible to trace throughout one sequence of thought or a consistent use of similes.

Observe the similar analysis in *ABC,* p. 1079*a.*

Commenting on the verse "And the sheep follow him: for they know his voice" (10:4*b*), both Macgregor and Strachan quote the following words of G. A. Smith out of the latter's own experience as a traveler in Palestine:

Sometimes we enjoyed our noonday rest beside one of these Judaean wells, to which three or four shepherds come down with their flocks. The flocks mixed with each other, and we wondered how each shepherd would get his own again. But after the watering and the playing were over, the shepherds one by one went up different sides of the valley, and each called out his peculiar call, and the sheep of each drew out of the crowd to their own shepherd, and the flocks passed away as orderly as they came.

Whom does John have in mind when Jesus speaks of "all that came before me" (v. 8) and when he says, "Other sheep I have" (v. 16)?

Reading 24: John 10:19-42
AT THE FEAST OF DEDICATION

1. Notice the reasons why some scholars, including the writer in *ABC* (see p. 1078*a*), regard the opening part of

this section as involving another case of mistaken arrangement within the Gospel of John. Do you agree that the putting of 10:19-29 after 9:41 makes for better continuity?

2. What was the origin and nature of the Feast of Dedication? See *ABC,* p. 1079*b*.

Whether the passage 10:19-29 belongs after or before the paragraph on the good shepherd, it can be interpreted only in close connection with that paragraph. Jesus is explaining the failure of many to follow him by pointing out that they do not belong to his flock and therefore do not know his voice. We do not need to accept any doctrine of election, in the Calvinist sense, in order to recognize the truth in these words. Only those who belong to Christ can understand his words.

Vv. 27-28*a* are a good text for a sermon. Observe the two parts of the sentence, each containing a reference to an act of Christ and an act of the Christian: (1) The Christian listens to Christ's words, and Christ "knows" him; (2) the Christian follows Christ, and Christ gives him eternal life (Macgregor). The word for "know" in this passage (and in the "good shepherd" discourse and elsewhere in this Gospel) means intimate personal acquaintance and understanding.

There follows another rather bitter controversy with "the Jews" and an attempt to arrest Jesus. But Jesus' hour has not yet come. According to the fourth Gospel, Jesus was not subject to men's wills in this matter: "No man taketh [my life] from me. . . . I have power to lay it down, and I have power to take it again " (10:18—A.V.). Thus on this occasion, as on previous ones, his enemies are unable to lay hands on him. He slips away from them, going across the Jordan into Perea. Look up Perea on the map in *ABC*. Many people believed on him there. As Macgregor reminds us, John likes to emphasize the faith of others—Samaritans and now Pereans—in contrast with Jewish unbelief (see above, p. 41).

Reading 25: John 11:1-16

RETURN TO BETHANY

1. Read Lk. 10:38-42, the only place in any of the Synoptic Gospels where the family, with which this great chapter deals, is mentioned. Note what details are added to our knowledge of the family by the Fourth Evangelist.

2. Why, would you say, did Jesus wait for two days after hearing of Lazarus' illness before starting to Bethany? Does the story give us any hint?

Jesus is presumably still in Perea when the news of Lazarus' illness reaches him. Whatever the reason for the delay of two days before responding to the sisters' appeal, the author makes it clear that it was not for lack on Jesus' part of love for the family. When he does start on the journey to Bethany (a village near Jerusalem), his disciples remind him of the danger there. But Jesus replies by telling them in effect that no one will be able to harm him as long as the Father has work for him to do. Just now the Father has work for him in Bethany. Therefore they must go there.

Jesus then tells them what this work is. "Our friend Lazarus is fallen asleep; but I go, that I may awake him out of sleep" (11:11*b*). We have observed how fond this writer is of exhibiting the dullness of "the Jews." They always take Jesus with absurd literalness. Here the disciples are represented as doing the same thing. Jesus has to enlighten them: "Lazarus is dead," he says, in effect; "and I am glad I was not there to prevent his death, because now I shall be able to give you sure evidence of my being the Son of God." Even so, they do not understand, for Thomas ("Didymus" means "twin") says to his fellows: "Let us also go that we may die with him."

Compare this reference to Thomas with that in Jn. 20:24-29. Is there a possible sermon here? The doubter can often, in conduct, be a man of heroic faith. Contrast this picture of Thomas with that of Peter, who affirmed his faith with such assurance but denied Jesus three times when there was danger of death.

Reading 26: John 11:17-44
THE RAISING OF LAZARUS

1. Do the characters of Mary and Martha as they are presented in this story agree with the picture of the sisters in the Lukan story (Lk. 10:38-42) ?

2. John places this story just before the final days leading up to the crucifixion. Do you see any reason why it serves his purpose to do so? Would the incident seem to him to be an anticipation of Jesus' own death and resurrection, so soon to take place?

This narrative, found only in John, is one of the great passages in the Gospel. The story is dramatically and effectively told. One has no trouble visualizing the incident, from its beginning in Jesus' conversation with Martha, who had gone out to meet him, to its end in Lazarus' emergence from the tomb with the graveclothes still on him.

Both Martha and Mary, when they first see Jesus, make the same prayer: "Lord, if thou hadst been here, my brother had not died" (vv. 21, 32). Jesus answers this prayer, first with words and the second time with his greatest miracle.

The words—with which he replied to Martha—are among the most moving in the Gospels: "I am the resurrection, and the life" (v. 25). The stress here is on the verb, and especially on its present tense. Jesus had said to Martha just a moment before: "Thy brother shall rise again" (v. 23), and she (failing, as so many do in this Gospel, to understand Jesus' true meaning) had said, "I know that he shall rise again in the resurrection at the last day." Then Jesus replied: *"I am* the resurrection, and the life." It is characteristic of the fourth Gospel to insist that "eternal life" is not something in the future; it is even now God's gift to those who have faith in Christ.

But Jesus' reply was not in words only. He asked to be led to the tomb where Lazarus had been buried for four days. (It was the Jewish custom to bury the body immediately after death.) "Four days" is emphasized (vv. 17, 39) in order to show the great wonder of the miracle; the body had already begun to decay.

Jesus' weeping, another evidence of his love for Lazarus, comes as something of a surprise in this Gospel, where the emphasis is so constantly on Jesus' divine power and nature. More in line with this usual character is the statement that Jesus prayed at the tomb not because he needed any special help but in order that the people might hear him and know that it was God who had given him the power to perform the great miracle.

Written Work.—Write out your conception of the meaning of the text: "I am the resurrection, and the life." In what sense is eternal life now available to us? What does that life consist in, and what are some of its marks?

Reading 27: John 11:45-57
THE PLOT TO PUT JESUS TO DEATH

1. Read carefully the brief summary of the significance of this section in *ABC,* pp. 1081b-82a.

2. Formulate in your own words what seems to be John's understanding of why the Jewish leaders were so bitterly hostile to Jesus.

We have already observed that John moves the cleansing of the Temple, which in the Synoptic Gospels takes place at this point in the narrative, to a point near the beginning of Jesus' ministry (see *Reading* 6). We can now see that one of the reasons for this transposition is that John understands the raising of Lazarus to have had the result which in the Synoptics is ascribed to Jesus' bold action in the Temple—namely, the bringing to a head of the hostility of Pharisees and Sadducees to Jesus.

See *ABC,* pp. 840 f., for the meaning of these party names. We can be all but certain that it was the Sadducees who took the lead in urging that Jesus be put to death, for they had a measure of political power under the Romans and stood to suffer most if the Romans, because of any disturbance, should take away the privileges the nation still enjoyed. John is thus supported by all we know of the political situation in Judea at this time when he attributes to Caiaphas, the high priest and a Sadducee (although John does not use the party name), the suggestion that Jesus be destroyed.

Caiaphas declared that it would be better for Jesus to be killed than for the whole nation to suffer the displeasure and the reprisals of the Romans; this would happen if this disturbing leader was not silenced. John sees in this statement a kind of unconscious, supernaturally inspired prophecy that Jesus through his death would become the Saviour of the world.

Ch. 11 ends with the stage all set for the dramatic final week: the Passover is near, which will bring Jesus to Jerusalem, where many of the people are eagerly waiting for him and where his enemies have plotted his death.

Reading 28: John 12:1-8
THE ANOINTING IN BETHANY

1. It is generally recognized that this story in John is based upon the similar story found in Mk. 14:3-9 (cf. Mt. 26:6-13). Observe the details which are added by John.

2. In both Mark and John this incident is narrated at the very beginning of the Passion story. Do you see any reason for this?

The Passover approaches, and Jesus has returned to the neighborhood of Jerusalem. He goes to Bethany, where his friends Martha, Mary, and Lazarus lived; and it is apparently in their home that the supper is being given, rather than in that of Simon the leper, as Mark has suggested. Efforts to harmonize the two stories in detail have not been very convincing. It is better to recognize differences in detail and to give one's attention to the essential content of the story, which is the same in the two Gospels.

Lazarus is mentioned in order that the reader may be

reminded of the miracle and may be informed that the man who had been raised from the dead was now living a normal life. One notices that the picture of the two sisters closely conforms to the Lukan characterization (10:38-42): Martha is serving, and it is Mary who anoints Jesus with the precious nard.

John gives a name also to the individual who most objected to this extravagance. Mark had said "some" were indignant and Matthew had identified them as disciples; John specifically identifies one man as the complainant, Judas Iscariot. He tells us also that Judas was a thief—an allegation which no other Gospel makes.

But Jesus defends Mary's act of devotion, reminding his disciples that they will not long have him with them. Mark's words are more moving than John's at this point: "She hath done what she could; she hath anointed my body beforehand for the burying" (Mk. 14:8).

Reading 29: John 12:9-19
THE TRIUMPHAL ENTRY

1. The triumphal entry is one of the very few incidents which are found in all four Gospels. Along with this passage read the parallels: Mk. 11:1-11*a;* Mt. 21:1-11, 14-16; Lk. 19:29-44.

2. Read Psa. 118:25-26 and Zech. 9:9 for the O.T. background of this story.

The triumphal entry is rather briefly described in the fourth Gospel, but it occupies an important place in the movement of the narrative. The greater brevity, in comparison with the other Gospels, is in considerable part explained by the Evangelist's omission of details as to how the colt was acquired on which Jesus rode into the city. John merely says, "And Jesus . . . found a young ass" (v. 14). Perhaps he took for granted in his readers some acquaintance with details from the other Gospels; more probably he did not regard them as important enough to mention.

Apparently the leaders in this demonstration of confidence were people who had come from Galilee and else-where to attend the feast. Many of them were probably living in improvised shelters in the environs of the city, but v. 18 informs us that many residents of the city itself came out to greet him as the Messianic King. Thus, it is clear that even for John many of "the Jews" believed on him, although in this passage he does not identify them as Jews. As we have seen, John usually reserves the name "the Jews" for Jesus' enemies.

We observe from the mention of Lazarus again in vv. 17-18 how very important John understands the effects of Jesus' great miracle to have been. We have seen that in connection with the Bethany anointing John mentions Lazarus; he does so again here. It is his view that this miracle of Jesus—John likes to call these mighty acts "signs"—precipitated the final crisis of the crucifixion.

The triumphal entry confirms Jesus' enemies in their belief that the only way to avoid a serious clash with the Romans is to destroy this man. The Synoptic Gospels do not connect the triumphal entry directly with the plot against Jesus, although Matthew comes close to doing so (Mt. 21:15f.). At this point John may well be more ac-curate: if the Romans, or their priestly associates, had wit-nessed anything like the triumphal entry, they would have felt more than justified in arresting Jesus. The political situation in Palestine was too "nervous" to allow for such a demonstration in honor of a possible "Messiah."

Reading 30: John 12:20-36
THE GREEKS SEEK JESUS

1. Read the critical comments on the passage in *ABC*, p. 1082b-83a, and the Scripture passages referred to there.

2. Read Mk. 14:34-40 (and parallels: Mt. 26:36-43; Lk. 22:40-46) and note differences from and similarities with Jn. 12:27-28.

As Macgregor points out, the triumphal entry has given the author an opportunity to remind us of the homage paid to Jesus by some of the Jews; here he shows us representatives of the Gentile world seeking to bring to him their tribute of praise. There can be no doubt that John sees a symbolic meaning in this incident: it is an anticipation of the success Christianity was to have among non-Jews.

The "Greeks" were Gentiles—we do not know from where—who had already become either actual proselytes to Judaism or, more probably, faithful friends of the synagogue ("God-fearers"). They had thus come up to the feast along with their Jewish neighbors. It is interesting to see that they approach Jesus indirectly. They speak to Philip, Philip speaks to Andrew, and the two of them bring the original request to Jesus (cf. Jn. 1:43f.). Notice that it is this desire of the Gentiles to see Jesus which alone interests the writer. He does not tell us whether these particular Gentiles saw him or not. Presumably they did; but that does not matter.

Jesus sees in this interest of the Gentiles in him the sign that the time has come for his death. All through the Gospel the writer has made no effort to conceal the hatred of many toward Jesus; but this hatred was always impotent to harm him—because his "hour" had not come. But now it *has* come; and no further concealment or "escape" on Jesus' part is to be expected.

Strachan writes:

The coming of the Greeks is the signal that the Spirit of Jesus is about to be set free on its world-wide mission. This can happen only through His death, resurrection, and return to glory by the divinely appointed way of suffering. . . . The words of vv. 23-26 are meant to make intelligible to the Hellenic Christian why Jesus actually devoted His mission on earth to Palestinian Jews. It was in order that He might die, in order to be "lifted up." . . . Jesus was slain by the Jews in order that he might become the Saviour of the world.

Paul has none of John's antagonism to "the Jews," but a somewhat similar understanding of God's providential use of Israel's rejection of Christ is expressed in Rom. 11:17f. But in Paul's view, Israel, too, will ultimately be saved.

Notice that Jesus speaks of his death as a glorification and an exaltation: the Son of Man is to be "glorified," to be "lifted up." Only if, through death, he returns to his Father, can the real harvest of his life be realized. "I, if I be lifted up, . . . will draw all men unto myself" (v. 32). This way of regarding the death of Christ—not as a tragedy redeemed only by the resurrection, but as being itself an exaltation—is unique in this Gospel. (See above, *Reading* 8.)

Vv. 27-28 come as near as John ever comes to giving us Jesus' agonizing prayer in Gethsemane. But how different! They say, in effect: "My soul is troubled. But shall I say, Father, save me from this hour? No; this is why I came to this hour. Father, glorify thy name."

The death for John is, as Vincent Taylor says, not a trial for Jesus nor a "scandal" to others but a "shining stairway" to the Father.

Reading 31: John 12:36-50
FAITH STRUGGLES WITH UNBELIEF

1. It is argued by many that we have in this reading another case of the kind of displacement we have seen often exemplified in this Gospel. The suggestion is that vv. 44-50 originally came before vv. 36-43. Does this suggestion appeal to you as being plausible?

2. Observe how excellent a brief summary of Jesus' teaching, as John understands it, are vv. 44-50. Pick out and formulate the several ideas and find earlier passages where they are more fully elaborated.

According to almost any way of outlining this Gospel, the passage we are now reading is the closing section of a major division. Jesus has been engaged in almost constant conflict with his enemies, who are now definitely set to destroy him if they can. This is the situation through ch.

12; but chs. 13-17 are devoted to an account of Jesus' last hours with his own disciples.

This passage, vv. 36-50, is obviously well adapted to concluding what Macgregor calls "the second act" of this drama, the act which presents "The Conflict of the New Gospel with the Old." It does two things: first (if we may take vv. 44-50 out of place), it gives us a summary of the grounds and meaning of the conflict which the writer has been describing and illustrating through several chapters and which is to reach its climax in the approaching cross; and secondly, it gives us a summary of the response of the people to Jesus' ministry.

One gathers that, in spite of all the signs of his mission which Jesus has given, the great mass of the people did not believe in him. As John saw them, they were perversely blind and refused to see the clear truth of God's revelation. Yet some did believe, even some of the leaders; but these for the most part were afraid to confess their belief. One thinks here of Nicodemus (Jn. 3:2) and of Joseph of Arimathea (Jn. 19:38). This distinction between a merely intellectual faith in Christ and real commitment to him is a suggestive and permanently relevant one.

Reading 32: John 13:1-20
JESUS WASHES HIS DISCIPLES' FEET

1. Read what was said in connection with *Reading* 17 about the absence of an account of the Lord's Supper in this Gospel; also *ABC*, p. 1084a.

2. Read Mk. 14:12-25 (and parallels: Mt. 26:17-29; Lk. 22:7-20), noting the difference between the Synoptics and John as to precisely when Jesus' last supper with his disciples was eaten.

This passage is notable for three principal reasons: the moving symbol of the mind of Christ which it contains in this act of loving, humble service; the light it throws upon John's understanding of the time of Jesus' crucifixion in relation to the Jewish Passover; and its omission of the institution of the Lord's Supper.

To consider the second point first: the Synoptists think of Jesus' last supper with his disciples as the Passover meal, which was regularly eaten on the evening of the fifteenth day of the Jewish month Nisan. John clearly believes this supper was an ordinary meal (as far as the Jewish calendar is concerned) eaten the day before the festival began. Thus, for the fourth Gospel, the death of Jesus took place at the same time as the killing of the Passover sacrifice: "Our passover also hath been sacrificed, even Christ" (1 Cor. 5:7b). This is one of several points where many scholars believe that John is probably more correct than the Synoptists.

Little needs to be said about the act of Jesus in girding himself with a towel and washing the disciples' feet; it speaks eloquently for itself. This service, in those days of sandals and dusty roads and streets, was often performed by a slave for one's guests. What better sermon could even Christ have preached on the text which he is shortly to give his disciples (Jn. 13:34): "Love one another; even as I have loved you"!

It is interesting to observe how true to Peter's character, as represented elsewhere in this Gospel and in the Synoptic Gospels also, is his conversation with Jesus in this story.

Not only is the account of the institution of the Lord's Supper omitted, but this story of Jesus' washing of the disciples' feet seems to be substituted for it. What is the meaning of this? One possible answer is that John is seeking to say to the church of his day, which may have been putting a false emphasis upon the outward rite merely as such, that the real meaning of the Supper was inner and spiritual communion. Says Scott (p. 123):

John wished in the most decisive manner to subordinate the outward rite to what was spiritual and essential. "By this shall all men know that ye are my disciples, if ye love one another." "Peace I leave with you, my peace I give unto you." Not a ritual ordinance, but the inward spirit of love, truth, peace, was Christ's real bequest to his disciples, by which they would be kept in fellowship with one another and declare themselves to the world.

It is this inward spirit that gives the Lord's Supper its reality and its supreme importance in the life of the church.

Reading 33: John 13:21-30
THE BETRAYER

1. Read the story of Jesus' remarks about his betrayer in the Synoptics (Mk. 14:18-21; Mt. 26:21-25; Lk. 22:21-23) and note the differences between the several versions of this story.

2. Why, do you think, did Jesus say to Judas, "What thou doest, do quickly"? Read *ABC* on this, p. 1084*a*.

3. Jot down for a sermon some of the ways in which Judas went into the "night" when he left the lighted room where Jesus sat with his disciples. This will not be "allegorizing"; John undoubtedly intends the statement to carry a symbolic meaning.

Jesus has just hinted that one of his disciples will be his betrayer (v. 18). Now he speaks more plainly: "One of you shall betray me." Mark (as well as Matthew, following Mark) describes how the disciples, deeply troubled by this solemn announcement, begin asking, "Is it I?" But Jesus does not tell them of whom he is speaking, unless Mt. 26:25 means that Judas was himself told that Jesus knew.

The story in John is fuller and even more dramatic. The disciples with Jesus are reclining, ancient style, at the table, leaning on their left elbows, with their right arms and hands free. One of the disciples, reclining on Jesus' right and therefore close to his shoulder, is asked by Peter to inquire who the betrayer will be. This disciple, who is not named, does so. Jesus replies, in effect: "The one to whom I shall give the piece of bread after I have dipped it in the dish." This was often done during a meal, so that only this disciple could understand the gesture when Jesus after dipping the bread gave it to Judas. Also only that disciple could have understood what Jesus meant when, looking at Judas, he said: "What thou doest, do quickly." When, having accepted the morsel from the Master, Judas left the room, he had made his final choice: "Then entered Satan into him" (v. 27). "And it was night" is, as we have said, not a mere note on the time; for the author it had great symbolic meaning (cf. 9:4 and 11:10). Strachan sees in the mention of the cockcrow after Peter's denial a point of conscious contrast to this reference to "night." For Peter there was hope (cockcrow came at the break of day); for Judas there was none.

Who was the disciple (was he the host?) who lay next to Jesus and heard his identification of Judas? He is described simply as one of the "disciples whom Jesus loved" (v. 23). On the question whether he could have been John, the son of Zebedee, see above, p. 22, and *ABC*, pp. 1065f. This is the first time in the Gospel this disciple is referred to, or at any rate is so described; but after this point he appears several times in the narrative.

Reading 34: John 13:31-38
THE NEW COMMANDMENT

1. In what sense is the commandment which Jesus here gives his disciples a "new" commandment? Read 1 Jn. 2:7f. and the comment on it in *Reading* 78 below.

2. Compare with Jn. 13:36f. the Synoptic accounts of the prediction of Peter's denial: Mk. 14:29-31; Mt. 26:33-35; Lk. 22:33-34*a*.

This brief passage falls into three parts. There is, first, another reference to Jesus' death as an "exaltation." The departure of Judas is a reminder that the "hour" has now fully come: "Now is the Son of man glorified" (v. 31). This glorification is to take place almost at once, so that his disciples will soon be looking for him and not finding him. (Later on in the Gospel he tells them that they will

69

not have to look long; as the Spirit, he will soon return and will be with them forever.)

The second part of the passage is devoted to the giving of a "new commandment": they are to love one another as Jesus has loved them. This is not a general ethical precept. It is not merely an affirmation of the duty of good will toward all men. Such a commandment would not have been "new." Jesus is referring to the peculiar love which must unite the members of the fellowship with one another. They must be bound to one another by the same love that Jesus has for them. This note will be struck several times again, especially in the prayer in ch. 17. The statement of Jesus that it will be the love of Christians for one another which will be the most conspicuous mark of the church reminds one of Tertullian's observation, a hundred years or so later, that the heathen were accustomed to exclaim with wonder, "See how these Christians love one another!"

The third part of the passage is concerned with the prediction of Peter's denial, which is a feature of all four Gospels. Peter, taking up Jesus' remark that where he was going his disciples could not come, asks with characteristic impulsiveness why he cannot go with Jesus even now, asserting that he is willing to die with his Master. Jesus silences him with the prediction of the denial.

Written Work.—Prepare a full outline of a sermon on vv. 34-35. One possible outline would be: (*a*) The nature of Christian fellowship; (*b*) the basis of Christian fellowship; (*c*) the witness of Christian fellowship.

Reading 35: John 14:1-14

THE WAY, THE TRUTH, THE LIFE

1. Many students of the fourth Gospel believe that chs. 15 and 16 originally preceded this chapter. Notice that ch. 14 ends as though it were the conclusion of a discourse. Read *ABC* on this, p. 1084*a*.

2. Observe how in this reading John again uses the literalmindedness of Jesus' disciples as a foil for the presentation of Jesus' spiritual meaning.

We begin now the reading of Jesus' final words to his disciples. Judas is gone and Jesus can speak intimately with his own. The result is one of the most eloquent passages in the whole of the N.T., John 14-16.

Jesus begins by comforting his followers about his death. They are to believe in God and in him. In the Father's presence (this is the meaning of "house") are many dwelling places—one for each of them. Jesus interprets his death as a going on ahead to get these dwellings ready for their occupancy. He will come back and will take them to be with him.

Jesus then says that he is the Way, the Truth, and the Life. To know him, in other words, is to be on the Way that leads to God; is to know the Truth about God; is, indeed, to enjoy already the Life which is in God. To see Christ is to see God, for Christ and God are one; and what Christ says and does is really what the Father is saying and doing in and through him.

The promise of Jesus that those who believe on him will do even greater works brings in a theme which will be developed more fully later in the discourse (see also *Reading* 30). He means that now he is limited in his work to the particular place where as a man he is standing, but after his death and his going to the Father he will be able to return as the Spirit, and as the Spirit he will be able to do more in and with and through his disciples than he is now able to do in and of himself.

It is in this connection that the promise about prayer must be interpreted. Jesus is thinking of the spiritual power which will be available to his disciples after his return to his Father—power always accessible to those who have faith.

Reading 36: John 14:15-31
THE HELPER

1. Notice that 14:30-31*b* sustains the suggestion that ch. 14 originally followed chs. 15 and 16.

2. On the basis of vv. 17-19, how would you formulate John's understanding of the relation of Jesus and the Spirit?

The giving of the Spirit, briefly touched on in the preceding section of this discourse, is now more fully set forth. His coming depends upon the disciples' loving Jesus and obeying his commands—especially, it is to be presumed, the command to have brotherly love for one another, the "new commandment." The world will not be able to receive this Spirit, this "Helper" (a better term than "Comforter"). Only members of the fellowship of believers will be able to discern his coming and to receive him.

Jesus then reveals that the Spirit's coming will really constitute his own return: *"I* will come to you" (A.V.). Readers of the Synoptic Gospels will remember that in those Gospels there is a lively sense of the future coming —the "second coming"—of Christ. In John only occasional traces of this so-called eschatological or apocalyptic belief can be found (14:3 seems to be such a trace). For the most part, John thinks of the resurrection and Pentecost as being the fulfillment of such hopes: Christ's "second coming" is the coming of the Spirit.

Jesus tells his disciples that after he is gone in the flesh the Holy Spirit will remind them of what he has said and been to them and will reveal to them the true meaning of what they can now only partly understand. We have here undoubtedly a clue to John's intention in his Gospel; he is seeking to present that true and inner meaning of Jesus' words and life which has become apparent only after Jesus' departure and under the influence of the Spirit.

"Peace be with you" was a conventional way of saying good-by. Jesus uses these words as he says farewell to his disciples (another evidence that this chapter belongs after

15 and 16), but points out that he is not using them in a conventional sense. He says, in effect, in v. 27a: "Not as the world says 'Peace' am I saying it. My own peace I give to you."

The reference to the "prince of the world" reminds us of the early Christian belief that this world was under the control of a demonic power and that Jesus met that power and conquered it on the cross.

Reading 37: John 15:1-16

THE VINE AND THE BRANCHES

1. Notice that Israel is often referred to in the O.T. as a vine (see Psa. 80:8-16; Isa. 5:1-7). Do you suppose that John is thinking of the church here as the new Israel? Is this what Jesus means when he says, "I am the *true* vine"?

2. How about a sermon on the power of Jesus' word (or message) as it is presented in this Gospel? Notice 15:3 in connection with 6:63 and 12:48. Christ's word is judging, cleansing, and life giving.

Here is another instance of the allegory—which, as we have seen, takes the place of the parable familiar in the Synoptic Gospels. This particular allegory is really—like Jesus' act of washing the disciples' feet—a sermon (in symbol) on the "new commandment" repeated here (v. 12): "Love one another, even as I have loved you." Just as a vine and its branches are united, so must Christ and his own be united. The evil branches—especially Judas—have now been pruned away; the remaining branches are expected to bear fruit. They *will* bear fruit if they stay in connection with Christ, who is the vine and the source of life and power.

This is a beautiful description of the Christian life as a life of love—the love of Christ for us and our responding love for him, and our love of one another within the fellowship, which is a phase of our love for Christ himself. Such a life of love bears righteousness as a kind of fruit. The true goodness is not the result of busy, tiring human effort, but

73

of God's creative power flowing through us as the sap flows through the branches of a vine.

Toward the end of the passage Jesus leaves the figure of the vine, but the emphasis is still upon the intimacy of his fellowship with his own: they are not his slaves but his friends; he has shared with them all he has received from his Father; he has chosen them and ordained them; he will soon be laying down his life for them.

Reading 38: John 15:17–16:15
THE WORLD AGAINST THE CHURCH

1. Would you say that this passage suggests conditions the church was meeting in the time of the author? How so?

2. It is proposed by some that vv. 26-27 are another instance of displacement. How plausible does this suggestion seem to you?

After another repetition of the command of mutual love, which is the real theme of these chapters, Jesus goes on to warn his disciples that persecution is to be expected. The church does not belong to the world, and the world cannot be expected to love those who are not its own. We have seen that the later books of the N.T. are all concerned, among other things, with helping the church in its fight against heresy within and its effort to withstand persecution from without (see above, pp. 15f.). In this passage, as occasionally elsewhere, the author of this Gospel is seeking to steel his readers against falling away from Christ under the blows of a hostile world. He tells them that Jesus, even when he was with his disciples, anticipated this persecution and prophesied that it would take place. Its coming is therefore a fulfillment of Jesus' prophecy and, far from shattering their faith, should strengthen their conviction that he is indeed the Christ.

Jesus says again that it is good for his disciples that he should go away. They are apparently so grieved at his announcement of his departure that it has not occurred to them to ask, "*Where* are you going?" (Macgregor). But it is Christ's destination which makes all the difference: he is returning to his Father, and from there will send the Helper, who could not come if Jesus had not first left. Strachan writes: "Exclusive interest today in the historic Jesus, as distinct from the risen and ascended Lord, still exemplifies this refusal to ask the question he desired his disciples to ask, 'Whither goest thou?' . . . We must not only follow his actions and ponder his recorded sayings while on earth. We must follow him in thought and faith."

We have seen that the Spirit's coming was understood by John as the fulfillment of the early church's expectation of Jesus' return; now, in vv. 8-11, he suggests that the final judgment has in effect already occurred in the Spirit's coming. The Spirit has come to judge as well as to save.

The passage closes with a repetition of an idea we have previously considered—one of the most fruitful and true of this writer's many great conceptions. This is the idea that the Spirit, when he comes, will take the words—and the life—of Christ and make their meaning plain. The revelation in Christ was not altogether complete in Jesus of Nazareth. The event had happened then, to be sure, but its meaning was not fully received. This inner meaning only the Spirit can disclose. That meaning the Spirit *does* progressively make known to those who yield themselves to Christ.

Reading 39: John 16:16-33
THE FINAL EXPLANATION

1. How would you state the meaning of prayer "in Christ's name"? Would vv. 26-27 suggest that it is not quite the same as prayer for "Christ's sake"?

2. In v. 25 "figures" is a better term than "parables" (that word, as well as the thing it stands for, as we have seen, is not found in this Gospel). The word used here covers any figurative or enigmatic way of speaking. Do you think we are meant to suppose that the disciples *really* understood and believed at this time? Compare with vv. 12-13 in this chapter.

This passage, according to the present arrangement of the Gospel, comes at the very end of Jesus' long discourse about the Spirit. The section begins with his disciples' expressing their perplexity and ends with their assertion that their doubts have all been cleared away and they fully understand and believe. But Jesus warns that there will still be difficulties to overcome.

Jesus has been explaining through 14:1–16:15 that he is going away to the Father, but that the Spirit will come to them and that this Spirit will be no other than his own living Presence. This is a reality of Christian experience (after the resurrection and Pentecost) and John's readers can understand it; but it is not surprising that Jesus' disciples, before his death, could not. Jesus' meaning could be only spiritually discerned—and the Spirit had not come. No wonder, then, that they are mystified and mutter to themselves: "What does he mean? Going away after a little while? Coming again after a little while?"

Jesus does not really resolve their perplexity. How could he? In the nature of the case, they could not understand his meaning then. He rather assures them that a meaning will soon be found; that whereas they will be stricken with grief when he leaves them, joy will quickly follow and they will then understand the meaning of what has occurred. There will be complete communion with God; the Spirit (the risen Christ) will not be a mediator merely, but will bring the believer into the very presence of God himself. Do you suppose, with Macgregor, that v. 21 is an enigmatic allusion to the birth of the church out of the agony of the crucifixion?

The disciples are apparently satisfied, and they profess their faith that Christ has come from God. But Jesus warns them that they will be scattered. Christ will be left alone to bear the cross. But on the cross he will overcome the world, and in that victory all who believe in him will share. We observe again the contrast and the conflict between church and world. The Christian belongs to both: in one he finds tribulation; in the other he finds security and peace. Strachan suggests that "Rom. 8:31-39 is one great answer to the promise of v. 33."

Reading 40: John 17
THE PRAYER FOR THE CHURCH

1. Before reading *ABC* or the comment below, read through this prayer of Jesus and make an outline of it.

2. Be especially careful to read *ABC* on this passage, pp. 1086-87.

3. Notice how many of the characteristic conceptions of the Gospel are expressed in this passage: Jesus' pre-existence; his commission to "reveal" the Father; the emphasis upon the church as separate from the world, upon the oneness of the church and the duty of mutual love, upon "eternal life" as consisting in "knowing" God and Christ, whom he has sent. Are there others?

This prayer of Jesus, often referred to as the "Prayer of Consecration" or the "Highpriestly Prayer," is the culmination not only of this "act" in the drama we are reading but also, in many ways, of the whole Gospel.

One notices from vv. 6-8 that Jesus thinks of himself as having now finished the work he came to do, even though his death has not occurred. This, as Macgregor points out, represents an advance theologically upon Paul, who apparently thought of Jesus' death as being the very center of his atoning work. For John the death is important, but in a different way. Jesus came to "reveal" God, to make him "known." He did this through his "teaching"—that is, through his disclosure of the truth about himself as the Son of God—and through his life. Of this revelation the death is only the culmination. His work was in principle complete before that final event, which John likes to think of as an "exaltation."

Observe how pervasive throughout the prayer is the understanding of salvation, or "eternal" life, as consisting in the knowledge of God and as being even now available. This "knowledge" was not mere intellectual comprehension but, as we have had occasion to see several times before, real communion and sharing of life.

As the prayer ends, Jesus thinks of those who first read this Gospel (in Ephesus, probably, about 100 A.D.) and also of us, who read it now, and includes us all in his intercession. The emphasis upon the oneness of the church reflects awareness of the threats to the church's life from internal schism as well as from the "world's" persecution. Both of these threats were very real when the Gospel appeared. Although the phrase is not used, we have here a mighty affirmation of the reality of the church as the body of Christ, the continuation of the incarnation.

Written Work.—Give a full outline of a sermon on Christian unity, using this passage as your source. Vv. 21f. would be a good text. You might discuss, among other things, the basis of Christian unity in the sharing of the one revelation of God in Christ and in the common experience of God's love expressed through and present in him. The idea (vv. 21-23) that it is through the oneness of the church that the heathen will be convinced of Christ's claims is important here (cf. 13:35). Is disunity keeping the church from bearing her true witness today?

Reading 41: John 18:1-27
THE ARREST OF JESUS

1. As *ABC* says (p. 1087*b*), from here on John follows the Synoptics more closely than before. Read the story of Jesus' arrest in Mark (14:32-52), Matthew (26:36-56), and Luke (22:40-53), noting down points of agreement and variation in the fourth Gospel.

2. Observe what *ABC* (pp. 1087*b*-88*a*) has to say about possible displacements or extraneous insertions in the story of Jesus' trial before the Jewish authorities. Virtually all commentators agree that there is some sort of dislocation in this passage. Does it seem so to you?

This reading falls into three parts: the arrest, the denial by Peter, and Jesus' hearing before the priestly authorities, with the second and third of these parts closely interlocked.

As one reads the Synoptic records of Jesus in Gethsemane in connection with John's account, one cannot fail to be impressed by two features of the Johannine story. The first is the absence of the agonizing prayer; the second, the absence of Judas' kiss. Both of these Synoptic items are omitted because they do not fit John's conception of Jesus. As to the agonizing prayer, note what was said earlier (p. 65) by way of comment on 12:27-28; observe also that v. 11*b* in this chapter is likewise derived from the Synoptic account of Jesus' agony, but is given a new meaning—a meaning consistent with John's conception of Jesus as being altogether beyond the reach of temptation. John would never have said, as Hebrews does (see below, p. 95): He was "in all points tempted like as we are" (Heb. 4:15). Thus, John omits any allusion to Jesus' bitter struggle in the Garden, just as at the beginning of his Gospel he omits any reference to temptation in the wilderness.

The kiss of Judas is omitted as not being fully consistent with Jesus' statement: "No one taketh [my life] away from me, but I lay it down of myself" (Jn. 10:18). Jesus does not need to be betrayed in the usual sense: "Jesus therefore, knowing all the things that were coming upon him, went forth, and saith unto them, Whom seek ye?" (Jn. 18:4).

The story of Peter's denial, which is interlocked with an account of preliminary hearings before Annas and Caiaphas, is told with a few new dramatic touches—as, for example, that Peter was warming himself at a charcoal fire when the denial took place. Because John does not tell that Peter later remembered Jesus' warning and repented with tears, the story in Mark is better adapted to preaching purposes; perhaps better adapted still is Luke's account, which includes the statement "The Lord . . . looked upon Peter" (Lk. 22:61).

The "other disciple" in this story is presumably the same as "the disciple whom Jesus loved." According to Garvie and others, he was a Jerusalemite disciple and the "Witness" whose experience lies back of the Gospel. But of this, as we have noted, one cannot be sure.

Reading 42: John 18:28–19:16
JESUS BEFORE PILATE

1. Read carefully *ABC* on this whole section, pp. 1088-89.

2. Note each of the indications of a disposition on Pilate's part to release Jesus. Observe that this emphasis upon Pilate's clemency in contrast to the people's demand for Jesus' death is another manifestation of the attitude toward the Jews which we have often noted in this Gospel.

3. Observe again signs that John thinks of the crucifixion as having occurred *before* the Passover.

4. Commenting on 18:40*b*, Strachan writes: "The sheer insincerity of the charge of sedition against Jesus is bitingly exposed." How is this true?

The Gospel story is now moving rapidly to its climax. After a hearing before the high priest Caiaphas, who, according to John, had first instigated the plot against Jesus (see above, p. 60), the Master is brought before Pilate, the Procurator of Judea. The seat of the Procurator was Caesarea (see map at end of *ABC*), but Pilate had come up to Jerusalem at the time of the Feast, when a disturbance was much more likely to occur than on ordinary days. The city was thronged with people from every part of the world.

John, who alone tells of a private conversation between Jesus and Pilate, conceives of the latter as eager to release Jesus, whom he does not understand, but whom he recognizes to be legally guiltless and politically harmless. Jesus makes at least an implied admission that he is a king, but affirms that his kingdom is the kingdom of truth. Pilate's question "What is truth?" is almost certainly asked ironically. Moffatt renders it: "Truth! what does truth mean?"— meaning "Truth is nothing that matters!" Jesus does not try to convince him by any argument. Those who know and love truth will understand and accept him; others cannot be convinced. These two figures, facing each other in private talk, make a dramatic picture. Which of them was really on trial? There is no end to the symbolic significance of the scene: political power against the power of truth; political interest against the will of God; empire against church; and so on.

It is most unlikely that Pilate was as innocent and "the Jews" as guilty as John supposes. The tendency to relieve the Romans of responsibility for Jesus' death and to place the blame on the Jews is understandable, as the Christian preachers moved into the Gentile world and the church became almost entirely non-Jewish. One can see this tendency operating from Gospel to Gospel, as we move from Mark to John. But the fact is that Pilate could not have been forced to crucify Jesus against his will. Besides, it is unlikely that one of the most ruthless governors Judea ever had would have been so concerned on behalf of this Jewish prophet. The Gospels have tried to relieve Pilate of a responsibility of which he probably did not think of trying to relieve himself. Although the connivance of the high priest and other leading Jews is not to be denied (see above, p. 63), it was the Romans who put Jesus to death. A clear knowledge of this fact will enable us to recognize and deny one of the falsest of the many rationalizations of anti-Semitism.

It is important to note that 19:13 is often mistranslated. The meaning is not that Pilate sat in the "judgment seat" but that he had Jesus sit there. Thus he can point to him and say, "Behold, your King!" Is this sincere, do you think, or ironical?

Reading 43: John 19:17-27
JESUS IS CRUCIFIED

1. Notice that Jesus is said to have carried his own cross. Can you think of any possible reason why John has departed from the Synoptics at this point? (See Mk. 15:21 and parallels, and *ABC*, p. 1089*a*.)

2. Observe any other features which are peculiar to the story of the crucifixion in this Gospel.

3. "Then therefore he delivered him unto them to be crucified. And they took Jesus and led him away" (vv. 16-17). To whom would you suppose the pronouns "them" and "they" refer? Does it not seem as though the people and their leaders did the crucifying? But notice v. 23.

4. Can you think of any reason why John should omit saying that the "two others" with whom Jesus was crucified were robbers?

John's story of the crucifixion follows the Gospel of Mark as closely as John ever follows anyone. Jesus, carrying his own cross—which was usual in these cases—is led to the place which, if it were outside one of *our* cities, we would call "The Skull." That is what "Golgotha" (Aramaic) and "Calvary" (Latin) mean. The Greek word here, in fact, is our word "cranium." It was apparently a hill outside Jerusalem whose shape suggested its name.

All four Gospels tell of Pilate's putting above the cross the inscription "The King of the Jews," but only John tells of the protest by the priests. Pilate refused to alter what he had written, doubtless being pleased with a title which well expressed the contempt he felt, less for Jesus himself, perhaps, than for the Jewish people, and which served to remind them that any "king" of theirs might expect the same fate at Roman hands.

Likewise, all four Gospels tell of the dividing of Jesus' clothes. But only John tells of the seamless tunic (undergarment). Is he thinking of the seamless garment as a symbol? Macgregor reminds us: "The full-dress of the High-priest (Exod. 28:31ff.), so Josephus tells us (*Ant.*, xi, 7, 4), was similarly seamless. Christ on the Cross is the world's High-priest (Heb. 3:1 and *passim*). Philo uses the High-priest's seamless robe as a symbol of the Logos . . . and Cyprian uses it as a symbol of the undivided Church."

More dubious probably is the symbolic meaning which many commentators (as, for example, E. F. Scott) find in the act of Jesus in entrusting the care of his mother to the "beloved disciple." This touching incident, which on any view John means us to take as a statement of simple fact, is interpreted as intended also to mean that Jesus' Jewish heritage has now become the possession and the care of the church. Jesus' mother passes into the house of his disciple; so Judaism is fulfilled in Christianity. In a Gospel as full of allegory as John's one cannot rule out such an interpretation, but it is far from certain.

Reading 44: John 19:28-42
THE DEATH AND BURIAL OF JESUS

1. Look up Psa. 22:18, Psa. 69:21, Ex. 12:46, and Zech. 12:10. These are the passages which John finds fulfilled in various details of the crucifixion story. Would you say that he makes a true use of Scripture? In what sense would you say that Christ's death *was* a fulfillment of Scripture?

2. Read carefully the paragraph on the crucifixion in *ABC*, p. 1089.

Jesus' thirst and the vinegar offered to assuage it are perhaps thought of by the author in connection with the "cup" God has given him to drink. The cup of vinegar is the symbol of the full measure of suffering he is bearing. With this suffering, his work is done. He cries, "It is finished!" and gives up his spirit. Notice that John wants to suggest even here that Jesus *gave up* his life of *his own accord*, just as he had earlier said, "No one taketh it away from me, but I lay it down of myself. I have power to lay it down."

This understanding of the death of Jesus as an entirely voluntary act John makes clearer by including the story of the soldiers breaking the legs of the other victims to hasten their death. When they come to Jesus, they find that he is already dead. Yes, he died—not because anyone killed him, but because it was the will of the Father that he should die and return to his own presence, his work having now been finished.

The quite gratuitous piercing of the side of the dead man is a poignant reminder of how brutal men can be. But

John tells us about it not on that account but in order that he may tell of water and blood flowing from the wound—symbolic, perhaps, of baptism and the Lord's Supper. Strachan prefers Burkitt's simpler explanation (from *The Gospel History and Its Transmission,* pp. 233f.) :

According to 1 Jn. 5:6-8 the living personality has in it three elements, viz. spirit, water, blood. From the "water" we are begotten, by the "blood" we are sustained, and the "spirit" or breath is the immaterial element that enters at birth and leaves at death. The spirit quitted Jesus when he died (Jn. 19:30), leaving behind the water and blood of a human body, the existence of which was demonstrated to the onlookers by the spear-thrust of the soldier.

If this explanation is accepted, the story becomes a further proof of the reality of Jesus' body and therefore an answer to the Docetists.

Ordinarily crucified criminals were left hanging. All the Gospels name Joseph of Arimathea as asking for permission to bury Jesus' body and as laying it in a rock-hewn tomb. Only John associates Nicodemus with him in this final act of love and reverence. These secret disciples forget their little fears in the presence of the Master's awful sacrifice.

Reading 45: John 20:1-18
JESUS APPEARS TO MARY

1. Compare this story with the corresponding sections of the Synoptic Gospels (Mk. 16:1-8; Mt. 28:1-10; Lk. 24:1-11). Lk. 24:12 is not to be found in the best and oldest texts of Luke.

2. Read 1 Cor. 15:3-8. What would this passage (written before any of the Gospels) suggest as to what was regarded as the more conclusive evidence for the resurrection—the appearances or the empty tomb?

John's story of the empty tomb is even more dramatic and moving than the Synoptic record. Mary Magdalene (does the "we" in v. 2 indicate that other women were with her, as the Synoptists say?) comes early on Sunday morning to visit the sepulcher. Observe that it is not said that she came to bring spices, because, according to John (19:39-40), Jesus' body was embalmed when it was buried.

When she sees the stone gone from the door of the sepulcher, apparently she takes for granted that the body has been stolen and runs to Simon Peter and the "beloved disciple" with the distressing news. One has no trouble in visualizing the scene: the two men running to the place; the (probably) younger man outrunning Peter and reaching the tomb first but hesitating to enter; Peter, characteristically, hesitating not at all; the silent contemplation of the linens so carefully arranged; the dawn of the truth that the Master has risen from the dead; the solemn departure with the august news.

The later scene is equally vivid: Mary, who knows nothing of this new resurrection faith, returning to weep at the grave; Jesus' appearance and their conversation, during which she gradually arrives at the same faith.

That she did not know the transfigured Christ until he spoke her name is a true and poignant detail of the story. The voice is in some ways the most intimate and authentic expression of the person. It is also perhaps the most persistent and constant. The passing years often make great changes in the appearances of our friends, but usually little in their voices. The resurrection body was not the same body Jesus had had before his death—it was that body wonderfully transformed—but the voice, especially when he spoke her name, was the same.

Reading 46: John 20:19-31

HE APPEARS TO OTHERS

1. Be sure to read *ABC* on ch. 20, pp. 1090-91.

2. Would you say that v. 31 adequately sums up what the author has actually done in the book we have been reading?

As the gospel spread into the Gentile world, there was an increasing tendency to emphasize Jerusalem in the career of Jesus. We have already noticed signs of this tendency in this Gospel. According to Mark and Matthew, the appearances to the disciples (not to Mary or the women) took place in Galilee; but Luke and John apparently suppose that they occurred in Jerusalem, where the disciples remained after the crucifixion.

John tells of two of these—the first when Thomas was absent and the second when he was present. On the occasion of the former of these Jesus does two important things: he formally ordains his disciples as his apostles ("even so send I you"—v. 21b); and he endows them with the Holy Spirit ("Receive ye the Holy Spirit"—v. 22b). Thus is Pentecost anticipated and Jesus' promise is fulfilled: "He shall give you another Comforter, . . . even the Spirit of truth" (Jn. 14:16b-17a).

The author includes the story of Thomas' doubt and of the decisive way Jesus answered it in order to refute the doubts which contemporaries in Ephesus or elsewhere often felt. Some of them were probably saying, "I wouldn't believe it unless I saw it." John replies, "That is what Thomas said when the resurrection was reported to him, but he ended by worshiping the risen Christ." This reference to the contemporary situation is clear from v. 29.

Vv. 30-31 were apparently intended to close the book, and there can be little question that at one stage the book ended at this point. The verses state the purpose of the Gospel: that we ("who have not seen") might be led to believe that Jesus is the Christ, the Son of God, and through believing might have life in his name.

Written Work.—Outline a sermon on v. 31, using some such topic as "The Faith That Brings Life." Does all belief issue in life? Note what James says on this (2:14f.). What is living and life-giving faith?

Reading 47: John 21:1-14
JESUS' FINAL APPEARANCE

1. Notice the grounds for regarding this chapter as an appendix to the Gospel (*ABC*, p. 1091*a*).

2. Observe also in the same paragraph of *ABC* the four reasons why, according to the commentator, the chapter was added by the "redactor." Read the whole chapter, noting the signs of the presence of each of these four motives.

3. Read Lk. 5:1-11, noting the points of agreement to which *ABC* calls attention.

It is interesting to observe that it is only in this chapter, certainly not a part of the original Gospel, that the Gospel of John speaks of "the sons of Zebedee" or hints that Jesus' more prominent disciples were fishermen. We have noticed a somewhat "aristocratic" interest in this Gospel; is this omission of reference to the vocation of Jesus' disciples a manifestation of this?

The incident involving Peter and "the disciple whom Jesus loved," which this chapter narrates, is typical of the relation in which these two stand throughout the latter part of the Gospel—ever since the "beloved disciple" was first mentioned. *ABC*, p. 1091*b*, says it well: "The beloved disciple has the quick discernment, but Peter, the swift action." Is not a good sermon suggested by this contrast? How futile is discernment without action; how futile—if not dangerous—is action without discernment! The church needs both disciples, and they need each other.

V. 12 again (like 20:14-16) suggests that Jesus, though recognizable, was not just as he had been. The resurrection body is a new body—a "spiritual," "glorious" body, as Paul says.

Reading 48: John 21:15-25
"FEED MY SHEEP"

1. In connection with Jesus' question in v. 15, read Jn. 13:37 and Mk. 14:29. To which of these accounts of Peter's

boast does the question of Jesus seem to look back?

2. Note, on page 1092a, *ABC*'s explanation of the occasion for including vv. 20-23. Does this seem to you a good explanation?

It is not clear that *ABC* is right in discounting the importance of the distinction between the two Greek terms for "love" which are used in Jesus' conversation with Peter, although both Macgregor and Strachan agree. One word might be described as meaning "reverential love," or "devotion"; the other, the more ordinary love of friendship. If, with Dr. Goodspeed, we translate the second word in its verbal form with the English term "to love" and the first with the phrase "to be devoted to," the conversation between Christ and Peter would run as follows:

"Are you devoted to me, more than these others are [as you claimed to be not long ago]?"

"I love you."

"Are you devoted to me?"

"I love you."

"Do you love me?"

"I love you."

It is not easy to suppose that this shifting of verbs has no significance. The reason Peter is grieved at Jesus' third question is not because of the repetition but because Jesus has altered his query and now seems to be questioning even Peter's statement (Goodspeed, *Problems of New Testament Translation*).

If "love" is the more affectionate term, and "devotion" the more deep-going and sacrificial, then "love" suggests just the quality of Peter's attitude up to this point, and "devotion" just the quality it has lacked. As the prediction of his martyrdom reminds us (vv. 18-19), the book of Acts shows us a Peter "devoted" as well as "loving." He *did* become a great shepherd of the church of God.

II

THE EPISTLE TO THE HEBREWS

AS we move from a reading of the fourth Gospel to the Epistle to the Hebrews, it is important to remember that we are moving backward in time. If we were considering the "later books" in strict chronological sequence we should take Hebrews first, for that document was almost certainly composed early in the nineties of the first century, certainly before 95 A.D. But there were obvious reasons for taking the fourth Gospel out of turn. From here on, however, we shall follow, as nearly as we can determine it, the chronological order.

The practical purpose of this Epistle is fairly clear. It belongs among those documents of the N.T. which are overshadowed by persecution or the threat of it. 1 Peter, which we shall read next, reflects the same kind of situation. The writer of Hebrews is troubled because the church to which he is writing does not impress him as being ready for the testing which is coming—which, indeed, may already have begun. The first ardor of its members has cooled, he fears. He is afraid that under the stress of persecution some of them will fall away, recanting their faith; perhaps a number of them had already done so. He writes, then, to remind them of how wonderful their religion is, how superior to all other religions, and therefore how amply deserving of their devotion and, if need be, the sacrifice of their very lives; to urge them by every possible appeal to continued loyalty to Christ; and to warn them most solemnly that apostasy, the denial of their profession, is really an unpardonable sin. As we read the Epistle we shall see that each of these notes is struck over and over again. You will remember that on p. 17 the last decade of the first century was men‚ tioned as one of the periods when persecutions of Chris‚ tians were especially severe and frequent, certainly in parts of the Empire. The book of Revelation almost surely was written in this period; and there can be little question that Hebrews was also.

There is pretty general agreement among students of the Epistle that although we cannot know the name of the great Christian thinker and preacher who wrote this docu‚ ment we can be fairly sure that its first readers were Romans. It would not be universally granted, however, that they were Jewish. Followers of this series have already been reminded several times that many of the first Christians thought of the church as the true Israel. The title The Epistle to the Hebrews may, therefore, have been given to this writing without any reference to race being in‚ tended at all. Besides, it should be remembered that the phrase "to the Hebrews" occurs only in the title (which would have been given to it only later), not in the text of the document itself, which begins without any address and less like a letter than a sermon or essay. The author, to be sure, says a great deal about Hebrew religion and makes large use of the O.T.; but that does not necessarily mean that his readers were Jews. He compares Christianity with Judaism in order to demonstrate its superiority to *all other religion,* of which Judaism was the highest ex‚ ample. But opinion on this point varies, as a reading of the introduction in *ABC,* p. 1295f., will indicate.

Again, as in the case of the fourth Gospel, it will be taken for granted that the student of these pages will have read this excellent introduction in *ABC.* Especially impor‚ tant are the paragraphs on "Philosophical Background," "A Philosophy of the Christian Religion," and "The Plan of the Epistle." Frequent reference to this "Plan" will help the reader follow the argument as he proceeds through the Epistle.

Commentaries by James Moffatt (*The Epistle to the He‚ brews,* Scribner's) and by T. H. Robinson (*Hebrews,*

Harper) may appropriately be added to the books on Hebrews which are mentioned at the end of the introductory essay in *ABC* on p. 1299. A very small book which I have found exceedingly helpful is *The Epistle to the Hebrews: Its Meaning and Message,* by James T. Hudson, published by T. & T. Clark, Edinburgh.

Reading 49: Hebrews 1:1:1–2:4
CHRIST IS ABOVE THE ANGELS

1. Read carefully the section "The Plan of the Epistle," *ABC,* pp. 1296*b*f.

2. Read through quickly 1:1-14; 3:1-6; 5:1-10; and 7:1–10:18. Do this in order to get an impression of the main argument of the book.

3. Note that the method of this author tends to differ from that of Paul in the handling of the "practical" materials. Paul usually has a practical section at the end of each of his letters; this author intersperses shorter practical sections throughout his Epistle. A theological section is regularly followed by some practical exhortation. Notice that this happens in the present *Reading.* Where does the practical section begin?

4. Look up the quotations used in 1:5-13. These are Psa. 2:7; 2 Sam. 7:14; Deut. 32:43; Ps. 104:4; 45:6-7; 102:25-27; 110:1. Do you believe that the author finds the meaning the original writers intended in these passages?

It has already been said that the principal object of this writer is to show the superiority of Christianity to any other religion. Since Judaism is, in his own judgment, the only conceivable rival, he is content to demonstrate its inferiority to the revelation in Christ. This object is disclosed in the very first sentences of the Epistle. After pointing out that the revelation in Christ has fulfilled and supplanted the revelation through the prophets, the author proceeds at once to show how much greater Christ is than the angels. He, like the later author of the fourth Gospel and possibly like Paul (see 1 Cor. 8:6 and Col. 1:15-17), thinks of the preexistent Christ as the Agent through whom God created and sustains the universe. Now, having redeemed us from sin, he has been exalted to God's right hand. He is as much greater than the angels as his name (Son of God) is greater than theirs (messengers of God). This claim is substantiated with a number of quotations from the O.T.

The little section 2:1-4 is one of the frequently interspersed sections of practical exhortation. If violations of the Old Covenant, given through angels and mere men, were faithfully punished, "how shall we escape" if we are unfaithful to the new revelation, which is bestowed in God's Son himself and is confirmed to us by the word of the apostles, by various miracles which they were enabled to perform, and by the Holy Spirit?

Vv. 1-4 give an excellent text for a sermon on the divine activity: the Creator and Sustainer of the Universe, the Saviour and the Judge of men.

Reading 50: Hebrews 2:5-18
THE NECESSITY OF THE INCARNATION

1. Notice the interpretation which this writer offers of the text of Psa. 8:4-6. Does it seem sound, or forced, to you?

2. Taking into account the use of Scripture found in this *Reading* and in the preceding one, how would you describe and evaluate this author's method of interpretation?

This passage is usually called a "digression," and in the sense that the writer has momentarily turned aside from the demonstration of the superiority of Christ and Christianity, this is true. Nevertheless, the section is of the greatest importance in the argument of the Epistle. In the first chapter, as we have seen, a very high conception of the divine nature of Christ has been presented; in the present passage the writer is concerned to emphasize not only how *real* was the *humanity* of Jesus but also how necessary that humanity was. He shows that the Son of God was compelled to become "very man of very man" in order to do what he did for our salvation.

The transition to the new theme is made by a reference to Psa. 8. In that psalm we are told that God has placed everything under man's feet. But, says this writer, that is obviously not true; man does not control all the world. It is then inferred that the allusion is not to man in general but to one man, Christ, who was made "for a little while" lower than the angels but has now been made Lord of all.

The reference to the temporary humiliation of the Son leads the writer to comment earnestly upon the necessity of it. Only by becoming fully human, even to the sharing of our sufferings and temptations, could Christ save us who are in bondage to sin and death. He could not become the Pioneer (Moffatt's term) of our salvation unless he came to the point where we ourselves stand. To lead us out of our bondage he must first identify himself with us in it.

As *ABC* reminds us, few, if any, N.T. writers have a higher conception of Christ's deity, but none lays a more telling emphasis upon the reality of his humanity or offers a more moving interpretation of its significance for us.

Reading 51: Hebrews 3:1–4:13
AN APPEAL FOR LOYALTY

1. Notice the outline of the sermon (3:7–4·13) in *ABC*, p. 1304*a*.

2. Observe in 3:6, 14 the emphasis upon loyalty and perseverance in the profession of Christianity. Remember what was said on pp. 16f., above, about the danger of falling away from the faith in this period.

In 3:1-6 the writer resumes his main theme. Having shown that Jesus Christ was greater than the angels, he now affirms Jesus' superiority to Moses.

In v. 1 the author refers for the second time (cf. 2:17) to Christ as the high priest. This is the writer's favorite way of thinking about the significance of Christ, and this theme is to be developed fully in the central section of the Epistle. These are only anticipatory hints of it.

Christ is superior to Moses because Moses *belonged* to the house (that is, to God's creation), but Christ *built* or *founded* the house (that is, was the agent of creation); besides, Moses was only a servant, but Christ was the Son. Has the "house" now become the "household," the church (see v. 6)?

After making this assertion, the writer again breaks off into a digression—this time a rather long one, 3:7–4:13—devoted largely to practical exhortation. As a whole, the passage seems to be a brief sermon, the text of which is Psa. 95:7-11. After quoting this text, the preacher warns of the dire effects of hardening our hearts against God's appeal, citing as an example the fate of those Israelites who perished in the wilderness. He then proceeds to show (4:1-13) that the promise of rest, made to these exiles and pilgrims in the desert, was not fulfilled to them and therefore is still outstanding. The rest, in other words, is still to be claimed by a people who will hear God's voice and not harden their hearts. The church is urged to be that people.

Written Work.—Read carefully the comment in *ABC,* pp. 1304-5, on 4:1-10 and 4:11-13. Fully outline a sermon on "The Urgency of Faith," emphasizing the elements of both opportunity and judgment which this whole passage stresses.

Reading 52: Hebrews 4:14–5:10

CHRIST OUR HIGH PRIEST

1. Read Phil. 2:6-11 and note that the writer's view of Christ is not very far removed from that of Paul. In Paul also we have a divine pre-existence, a real and sacrificial humanity, and an exaltation at the resurrection.

2. Read Gen. 14:18-20 and Psa. 110. This is the only scriptural basis this author has for his view that Jesus Christ is a high priest after the order of Melchizedek. Would you say that the basis is sufficient?

The section 4:14-16 constitutes the conclusion of the sermon we have been examining, but it also serves to introduce the major theme of the Epistle, namely, the high priesthood of Jesus. This passage lays a wonderful basis for a sermon on the meaning of Christ for the believer. We can approach God with confidence because we know that in Christ he has known and shared our limitations. Christ is able to *sympathize* with us in our temptations because he was tempted in *every point* just as we are tempted; but he is able to *help* us, as the high priest of Israel was not, because he has actually "passed through the heavens" into the very presence of God.

In 5:10 Dr. Moffatt (in *The Epistle to the Hebrews*) finds the following arrangement:

I. The high priest must be
   (a) sympathetic with those who sin, since he is human and sinful also (vv. 1-3),
   (b) not self-appointed to his task, but appointed by God (v. 4).
II. So Jesus was
   (b) not self-appointed (vv. 5-6).
   (a) able to sympathize because he suffered as a man (vv. 7-10).

No more moving account of the suffering and weakness which Christ assumed in order to become our Saviour can be found, either in the N.T. or outside of it, than vv. 7-10. Vv. 8-9 make another good text—this book abounds in them —for preaching on the meaning of Christ for the Christian. In v. 10 reference is made again to Jesus' priesthood being after the order of that of Melchizedek—a matter to which the writer will return soon again for more extended discussion.

Reading 53: Hebrews 5:11–6:20
THE DANGER OF FALLING AWAY

1. Do vv. 11-12 throw any significant light upon the date of this Epistle?

2. Read 6:4-8 and the explanation in *ABC* (pp. 1307*b*f.).
What conditions in the writer's period were likely to pro-
duce lapses from the faith?

The author having twice referred to Christ's Melchizedekian priesthood, we might well expect him to explain
what he means. This he intends to do (7:1–10:18), but he
is still not quite ready for that. He interjects here another
section of practical exhortation, explaining that it is hard
to discuss such a matter as the Melchizedekian priesthood
—which he admits is rather obscure—with such immature
Christians as the readers of this letter.

Dr. Goodspeed finds a great deal of significance in 5:12:
"You ought to be teaching others instead of needing to be
taught yourselves." In that scholar's opinion, the response
of the Roman Church to this rebuke is represented by 1
Peter (see below, pp. 108f.) and 1 Clement, an epistle
sent by the church at Rome to the church at Corinth at
about this same time (c. 95 A.D.). This suggestion of Dr.
Goodspeed's is interesting and by no means improbable.

Ch. 6 begins with an exhortation that the readers of the
Epistle go on beyond the elementary doctrines they have
learned—teachings about such matters as repentance, faith
in God, baptism, the resurrection, and the judgment—to
more mature matters, such as the interpretation of Christ's
high priesthood, which the writer wishes to discuss with
them. The chapter ends with a renewal of emphasis upon
the promise of God to those who are faithful, a promise
well exemplified by God's promise to Abraham. As *ABC*
suggests, the final sentence of the chapter serves skillfully to
bring the discussion back to the main theme again, Christ's
Melchizedekian priesthood.

Reading 54: Hebrews 7
THE MELCHIZEDEKIAN PRIEST

1. Read carefully the excellent summary of this chapter
in *ABC,* pp. 1309f.

2. Notice how much meaning the writer is able to derive

from the meager statements of Gen. 14 about Melchizedek. He does this by finding an allegorical significance in the Bible text. What do you think about the propriety of using Scripture in this way? Read *ABC*, p. 1310*a*.

3. Go through this chapter and list all the respects in which Christ is found to be superior to the Levitical priest.

The section begins by recalling the story of Genesis about how a priest named Melchizedek met Abraham as he returned from battle and received from him a tenth part of the spoils. He must have been greater than Abraham, this writer infers, since it was he who received the tribute, not Abraham. But others besides Abraham made this acknowledgment; the whole Levitical priesthood, which would later be created, was represented by Abraham, the writer argues, in this act of obeisance (vv. 9-10).

"Melchizedek" means King of Righteousness, and he is called King of Salem. Since "Salem" means "peace," the writer infers that this priest was supremely characterized by righteousness and peace; and since Genesis says nothing about his parents or about when he was born or when he died, it is assumed that he had no parents and was not born and did not die at all!

I think we would probably all agree that this writer got more meaning out of these few verses in Genesis than he should have; but this way of interpreting Scripture was highly regarded in his day, at least in some quarters. That he was not the first to allegorize this particular bit of Scripture is shown by Psa. 110:4, upon which the writer to the Hebrews was somewhat dependent.

This ancient priest, Melchizedek, so many generations earlier than Levi and Aaron, is seen by this writer as a type of Christ, the supreme High Priest. As Melchizedek antedated, so Christ has supplanted, the Levitical priesthood. The remainder of this *Reading*, and indeed of the whole section down to 10:18, is devoted to demonstrating the superiority of Christ's divine priesthood to any earthly priesthood. You will have noted the several points in this demonstration. Probably the most important of these is that the sacrifices offered by the earthly priests have to be repeated again and again, whereas Christ's sacrifice was made once and for all. Also, other priests offer sacrifices of various kinds; our High Priest has offered himself.

Reading 55: Hebrews 8
THE TRUE TEMPLE AND THE NEW COVENANT

1. Read vv. 1-5, together with the comment on the verses in *ABC,* pp. 1312*b*-13, noting especially the signs of Plato's influence on the author to the Hebrews. The influence is pervasive, as we shall see.

2. Vv. 6-13 introduce the idea of a new covenant. Read *ABC* on this passage (p. 1313) and compare what Paul has to say about the covenant in Gal. 3, especially vv. 15-17.

Continuing his demonstration of the superiority of Christianity to Judaism, the writer now makes the point that it has a superior tabernacle (vv. 1-5) and represents a higher covenant (vv. 6-13).

In connection with what he says about the tabernacle, we have occasion to observe a characteristic of his thought which we have not yet considered in the course of these *Readings,* although it really pervades the whole book and has been discussed in the Introduction in *ABC.* This characteristic is the habit of looking upon the actual world of the sense as being only a shadow of the real world, which is spiritual and heavenly. In this the author shows the influence of Greek thought, and especially of Plato. In the present instance, the point is that the tabernacle of Moses was but the material shadow of the real tabernacle, which is in heaven. Into *that* tabernacle Christ has now gone to fulfill his functions of high priest. Compare this with the statement of Jn. 4:21f.: "The hour cometh, when neither in this mountain, nor in Jerusalem, shall ye worship the Father; . . . but . . . when the true worshipers shall worship the Father in spirit and truth."

But not only does Christ, the supreme High Priest, officiate in the supreme temple, he also administers a new and supreme covenant. Judaism was thought of as a covenant between God and his people—certain duties were assumed by the people and certain promises were made by God. This covenant was usually associated with Moses and the Law. Paul, a generation earlier than our author, had made much of the fact that the covenant was made with Abraham, centuries before Moses and the giving of the Law, and that, therefore, this ancient agreement was not based upon Law, but upon faith on man's part and grace on God's. This writer, with the same end in view, makes a somewhat different point: he cites the O.T. itself (Jer. 31: 31-34) to show that even before Christ's coming the inadequacy of the old covenant, based on Law, had been recognized. The new covenant written on the heart, which was announced by the prophets, has now been bestowed in Christ.

Reading 56: Hebrews 9:1-14
THE MINISTRY OF CHRIST

1. Notice the excellent outline of this chapter in *ABC,* p. 1314*a.* Read this whole chapter through with this outline before you.

2. It is significant that the writer bases his argument upon the description of the tabernacle in the book of Exodus (notice references in *ABC,* p. 1314) rather than on the actual Temple at Jerusalem. Does this fact have any bearing on the question of the date of the Epistle? Does it also suggest that this writer's knowledge of Judaism was derived from the O.T. rather than from the practices of a contemporary Jewish community?

3. Read the final paragraph in the comment on vv. 6-10 in *ABC,* p. 1315*a.* There is no question that this summary of why Judaism failed is a fair representation of the thought of the writer to the Hebrews. But would you say that it is altogether fair to Judaism? How about some of the psalmists and the prophets? The priestly system was not the whole of Hebrew-Jewish religion.

Returning now to the conception of the better sanctuary introduced in the preceding chapter, the writer discusses at greater length the superiority of the heavenly tabernacle and Jesus' sacrifice within it to the earthly tabernacle and its ministries. There is a summary description of the arrangements and contents of the tabernacle (read comment on vv. 1-5 in *ABC*, p. 1314). The writer evaluates the worship there, noting especially that it was concerned only with outward regulations as to food, drink, and the like. It brought only a bodily purity.

But now Christ, the Melchizedekian High Priest, has entered into the eternal tabernacle with the offering of his own blood, and through that unique, supreme, and unrepeatable sacrifice has cleansed our consciences "from dead works to serve the living God" (9:14*b*).

Written Work.—Using 9:14, prepare a full outline of a sermon on "The Sacrifice of Christ," pointing out the uniqueness of the sacrifice (he offered *himself,* and the sacrifice was without *any* spot or blemish) and the uniqueness of the effect (cleansing of conscience and power of service).

Reading 57: Hebrews 9:15–10:18
CHRIST'S DEATH AND THE NEW COVENANT

1. For the story of the establishment of the "first" covenant, to which the writer refers here, see Ex. 24:4-8.

2. Define the two senses in which the word "covenant" (or "testament") is used in vv. 15f. (see *ABC,* p. 1316*a*). Do you see that both meanings apply in the case of Christ? In what senses did Christ make us the beneficiaries of his *will?* In what senses did he bring into existence a new *agreement* between men and God?

With this section the author brings to a conclusion his great theological argument—his description of Jesus' high priesthood. The passage is really a further elaboration of the ideas, already presented, of Jesus' supreme ministry to men and of the new covenant which God through him has now made with men.

The author begins with an attempt to show that the death of Christ was essential to the new covenant. One of the most persistent problems of the early Christian teachers was to explain why Christ had to die. That he had suffered death upon the cross was too well known to be doubted. It was instinctively felt that this death had something essential to do with the forgiveness of sins which the church had experienced and with the hope of final salvation in which it rejoiced. But just how did Christ's death bear on this experience and hope? Followers of this series have seen how Paul at various times answers this question. The author of the Epistle to the Hebrews has an answer of his own.

He points out that there cannot be a covenant in any sense without the death of some person, or of some living thing, being involved. A will, or testament (one meaning of "covenant"), is not valid until the maker of it dies. Likewise, the old covenant (in the sense of "agreement") was sealed with the blood of animals, and under it various washings and sprinklings with blood were required. This argument may seem to us a little forced, but it was strong enough to convince the author that there can be no covenant of any kind without the shedding of blood. The new covenant must, therefore, be sealed with blood. And it has been so sealed. Christ entered the heavenly sanctuary and offered one effectual sacrifice, his own blood.

The need for the shedding of blood is likely to seem less clear to us than to the ancients, who found it difficult to think of forgiveness of sins, or even of worship, except in connection with animal sacrifice. But the sense of the seriousness of sin which is expressed in this way is an abiding experience. God freely forgives us, but the forgiveness is not a soft indulgence. It is incalculably costly to God. This is really what the writer is saying when he speaks of Christ as the High Priest who offered his own blood as a sacrifice for sin.

In 9:28 we are reminded that although this writer happens not to say a great deal about the second coming of

Christ he is thoroughly persuaded of it. The same expectation is suggested by 10:13.

Reading 58: Hebrews 10:19-39
THE CHRISTIAN LIFE

1. Outline a sermon or prayer meeting talk on vv. 22-25 on "The Christian Life." Emphasize "true heart," "full assurance of faith," "cleansed conscience," "unwavering hope" (this is really the word here, not "faith"), "love and good works"; and bring out the meaning in relation to these of baptism (v. 22) and "the assembling of ourselves together" (v. 25).

2. In the light of vv. 35-39, how would you distinguish between the meaning of "faith" for Paul and for the writer?

Having completed his argument, the writer now turns to exhortation. The rest of the Epistle is largely devoted to practical instruction and to repeated appeals to loyalty and repeated warnings against apostasy. This particular *Reading* falls into three sections: vv. 19-25, 26-31, and 32-39.

The first of these little sections, following immediately upon the main argument, draws the conclusion that since we have so many privileges as Christians (a "new and living way" to God's presence, and a perfect High Priest and Mediator) we must not fail to make full use of them. Let us "draw near" to God. The conditions of our doing so are sincerity, faith, hearts sprinkled clean (that is, forgiven), and, apparently, baptism. Further we must not let our hope of final salvation waver, we must encourage one another to love and good deeds, and we must not neglect meeting together. These injunctions might be addressed to modern Christians just as appropriately as to these first century believers.

In the next section, vv. 26-31, the author again states his doctrine that there is no saving repentance after apostasy. The question whether one who denied the faith (as under persecution) could, under any conditions, be received back into the church again was to be a matter of controversy for generations, especially in the periods when persecution was most severe. The writer to the Hebrews answers that question with a decided No. This will seem to us a harsh teaching, but it simply reflects the serious view this writer took of the sin of deliberately denying Christ. Besides, it must be remembered that he is speaking not to penitent apostates but to Christians who might more easily give way to temptation if they believed a way back into the fold would be opened to them. A practical motive thus reinforced the writer's judgment that for this sin, at least, an adequate penitence was impossible.

This *Reading* ends with a renewed appeal to loyalty to Christ and to patient confidence ("faith") in God's ability and readiness to bring to pass the salvation he has promised.

V. 34 in the A.V. contains a reference to the writer himself. This is not found in the better, more ancient MSS., and does not appear in the better texts and translations. The verse should read: "Ye both had compassion on them that were in bonds . . ."

Reading 59: Hebrews 11:1-31

HEROES OF FAITH

1. This chapter (including the next *Reading*) is one of the greatest passages in the Bible. Read through the whole (11:1–12:2). If anyone decides to commit the whole to memory, he will never regret having done so.

2. Is your previous statement of what this writer means by "faith" borne out by this chapter?

3. Read carefully *ABC* on this passage, pp. 1319-20.

Ch. 11 of Hebrews together with 12:1-2, which belongs integrally with it (see next *Reading*), is a unit, and it is somewhat arbitrary to divide the passage. It is broken into two *Readings* only to encourage more careful study of the entire passage.

The passage begins with a definition of faith. Note that for this writer "faith" is *confidence* that God's promises will

103

be fulfilled. Such assurance would be particularly important for people whose loyalty was being put to the test by persecution. The author then goes on to illustrate the meaning of this faith and to lay the duty of it on the hearts of his readers by citing the examples of the heroes of Israel. (Notice how completely these heroes have been appropriated by the church, the new Israel.)

One observes that in almost every case the emphasis falls upon the hero's confidence in God's reliability in fulfilling what he has promised. Noah believes and acts on God's warning "concerning things not seen as yet" (v. 7). Abraham goes out to a place "which he was [afterward] to receive for an inheritance" (v. 8). Sarah "counted him faithful who had promised" (v. 11). Abraham so trusted God as to be ready to offer up in sacrifice the very son through whom, as he understood it, the promise to him was to have been fulfilled, "accounting that God is able to raise up, even from the dead" (v. 19). The same confidence is emphasized in connection with Moses, as the italicized passages in *ABC's* discussion, pp. 1320-21, show.

Written Work.—Outline fully a sermon on Heb. 11:27, discussing "The Meaning of Faith," as (1) decision between opposing values, (2) courageous action, and (3) patient endurance through trust in the Invisible God. Or perhaps you will wish to use some other outline.

Reading 60: Hebrews 11:32–12:2

HEROES OF FAITH

1. Observe how well adapted this passage is to encouraging the Christians to loyalty in persecution.

2. Are those who are said to surround us, in v. 1 of ch. 12, merely "witnesses"? Would you not say, in the light of 11:39-40, that they are thought of as having an anxious interest in our fidelity?

3. Read carefully the discussion of 12:1-2 in *ABC*, p. 1322a; then note in the verses the skillful use of the metaphor of the arena. This should suggest a sermon.

Thus far the writer has been dealing severally with these heroes of faith. Now, as he approaches the peroration of this eloquent passage, he names many together and refers to multitudes of unnamed heroes who, because their confidence in God was firm and strong, were able to suffer indescribable hardships and to perform amazing deeds. Note the suggestions in *ABC*, p. 1321*b*, as to who some of these unnamed persons probably were.

In vv. 39-40 the writer sums up the whole chapter by saying that, although these elders "obtained a good report" —that is, reputation—by their loyalty, they have not yet reached the goal they sought. They are still, so to speak, waiting for the reward of their faith. That reward is the salvation in Christ, which is very soon to come. God has held that reward back so that we, too, might enter into the possession of it—that "apart from us they should not be made perfect" (v. 40).

Surrounded as we are with this great cloud of witnesses, says the writer, let us run with patient endurance the race that is set before *us*. And then he brings this great passage to an end with a reference to Jesus the Lord, the "author and perfecter of our faith" (12:2; cf. 2:10), who "for the joy that was set before him endured the cross, despising shame" (v. 2).

Reading 61: Hebrews 12:3-29
VARIOUS ADMONITIONS

1. Read the passage through, noting what seem to you to be the topics dealt with.

2. Compare 12:12-17 with 6:4-6 and 10:26-27, remembering the relation of the teaching to the situation of the church which this writer is addressing.

This *Reading* falls into four parts. There is, first, a short comparison (vv. 3-4) of the sufferings the readers of the Epistle are undergoing or may have to undergo with those of Christ. Beside his sufferings, theirs are small indeed. He

105

gave his life; they have not yet been required to give nearly so much.

The writer then goes on to discuss the value of their sufferings as discipline (vv. 5-13). Christ, we remember, was, according to the writer, "made perfect" through suffering (Heb. 5:8-9). We too cannot expect to grow spiritually except as we accept patiently the same discipline. We are likely to think here of such passages as Rom. 5:3-4 (A.V.): "We glory in tribulations also: knowing that tribulation worketh patience; and patience, experience [or character]." V. 11 is a useful reminder that experiences which at the moment give us greatest pain can often be looked back to gratefully. The remembrance of this fact can often help us when we are in the midst of our difficulties and sorrows.

In vv. 14-17 the writer recurs to a theme often dealt with in the Epistle: the fact that one who falls from grace through apostasy cannot be restored. Here he recalls the example of Esau as a kind of proof of his position. Esau "found no place of repentance, though he sought it carefully with tears" (A.V.).

The rest of the chapter is devoted to a final brief description of the two covenants (see *ABC,* p. 1323*b,* for the exegesis of a rather difficult passage). The Christian who rejects the covenant offered in Christ may expect a more severe judgment than those who forsook the lesser covenant of Moses, just as fidelity to it will bring a more wonderful reward.

Reading 62: Hebrews 13
FINAL MORAL APPEALS

1. Read the passage through, jotting down the topics dealt with.

2. Would you take v. 24 to mean that the writer is writing *from* Italy or *to* Italy? Both answers have been given. Observe also that this Epistle, while it ends like a letter, does not begin like one.

3. Is not v. 7 enough evidence that Paul could not have written this Epistle?

4. On the very difficult passage 13:9b-16, see *ABC,* p. 1325.

5. Memorize the benediction, 13:20-21.

This passage, except for 9b-16, raises no difficult questions for the interpreter. There are counsels about love of the brethren, hospitality, care for prisoners (this will mean "prisoners for Christ's sake") , marriage, and about the peril of love of money. On the last of these topics the Epistle strikes the same note as Jesus' own teaching strikes (in Mt. 5:19f.) : God will provide for us. Thus covetousness is not only a wicked selfishness but also a denial of faith in God.

There follows a reference to the unnamed founders of the church addressed. If that church is Rome, Peter and Paul may well be in the author's mind, for they were the reputed founders of that church. V. 8 ("Jesus Christ the same yesterday, and today, and forever"—A.V.) falls between this allusion to the founders and a warning against new doctrines. The same Christ who was known to the founders is known to us and will be known to our children.

In v. 17 the writer returns, after a digression, to the subject of the church's leaders—this time its present leaders —and urges obedience to them on the part of the members of the community. In that connection the writer speaks for the first time in the first person, asking for the congregation's prayers. A beautiful benediction and some further personal remarks conclude this great document of the first century church.

III

THE FIRST EPISTLE OF PETER

EARLY in this book I referred to a letter of Pliny which has great importance for an understanding of the attitude of the state toward early Christianity. Pliny was a Roman who served a brief term as governor of the combined provinces of Bithynia and Pontus in Asia Minor, when Trajan was the emperor. The following letter, written in or near 110 A.D., was addressed to the emperor:

It is a rule, Sir, which I inviolably observe, to refer myself to you in all my doubts; for who is more capable of guiding my uncertainty or informing my ignorance? Having never been present at any trials of the Christians, I am unacquainted with the method and limits to be observed either in examining or punishing them. Whether any difference is to be made on account of age, or no distinction allowed between the youngest and the adult; whether repentance admits to a pardon, or if a man has been once a Christian it avails him nothing to recant; whether the mere profession of Christianity, albeit without crimes, or only the crimes associated therewith are punishable—in all these points I am greatly doubtful.

In the meanwhile, the method I have observed towards those who have denounced to me as Christians is this: I interrogated them whether they were Christians; if they confessed it I repeated the question twice again, adding the threat of capital punishment; if they still persevered, I ordered them to be executed. For whatever the nature of their creed might be, I could at least feel no doubt that contumacy and inflexible obstinacy deserved chastisement. There were others also possessed with the same infatuation, but being citizens of Rome, I directed them to be carried thither.

These accusations spread (as is usually the case) from the

mere fact of the matter being investigated and several forms of the mischief came to light. A placard was put up, without any signature, accusing a large number of persons by name. Those who denied they were, or had ever been, Christians, who repeated after me an invocation to the Gods, and offered adoration, with wine and frankincense, to your image . . . and who finally cursed Christ—none of which acts, it is said, those who are really Christians can be forced into performing—these I thought it proper to discharge. Others who were named by that informer at first confessed themselves Christians, and then denied it; true, they had been of that persuasion but they had quitted it, some three years, others many years, and a few as much as twenty-five years ago. They all worshipped your statue and the images of the Gods, and cursed Christ.

They affirmed, however, the whole of their guilt, or their error, was, that they were in the habit of meeting on a certain fixed day before it was light, when they sang in alternate verses a hymn to Christ, as to a god, and bound themselves by a solemn oath, not to any wicked deeds, but never to commit any fraud, theft or adultery, never to falsify their word, nor deny a trust when they should be called upon to deliver it up; after which it was their custom to separate, and then reassemble to partake of food—but food of an ordinary and innocent kind [Christians were often accused of eating human flesh in their meetings]. Even this practice, however, they had abandoned after the publication of my edict, by which, according to your orders, I had forbidden political associations. I judged it so much the more necessary to extract the real truth, with the assistance of torture, from two female slaves, who were styled *deaconesses:* but I could discover nothing more than depraved and excessive superstition.

I therefore adjourned the proceedings, and betook myself at once to your counsel. For the matter seemed to me well worth referring to you—especially considering the numbers endangered. Persons of all ranks and ages, and of both sexes are, and will be, involved in the prosecution. For this contagious superstition is not confined to the cities only, but has spread through the villages and rural districts; it seems possible, however, to check and cure it. 'Tis certain at least that the temples, which had been almost deserted, begin now to be frequented; and the sacred festivals, after a long intermission, are again revived; while there is a general demand for sacrificial animals, which for some time past have met with but few purchasers. From hence it is easy to imagine what multitudes may be reclaimed from this error, if a door be left open to repentance.

Trajan's answer to this letter was as follows:

The method you have pursued, my dear Pliny, in sifting the cases of those denounced to you as Christians is extremely proper. It is not possible to lay down any general rule which can be applied as the fixed standard in all cases of this nature. No search should be made for these people; when they are denounced and found guilty they must be punished; with the restriction, however, that when the party denies himself to be a Christian, and shall give proof that he is not (that is, by adoring our Gods) he shall be pardoned on the ground of repentance, even though he may have formerly incurred suspicion. Informations without the accuser's name subscribed must not be admitted in evidence against anyone, as it is introducing a very dangerous precedent, and by no means agreeable to the spirit of the age.[1]

Now if the reading of these letters is followed by a perusal of 1 Peter, it will at once appear that this Epistle is looking from inside the church at just such a situation as Pliny's letter contemplates from the Roman point of view. There is correspondence even as regards place, for Pontus and Bithynia, where Pliny was governor, are among the provinces to which I Peter was sent.

May not there also be correspondence as to time? May 1 Peter not have been written during Trajan's reign? Many scholars think so. Others put it in the same period as Hebrews and Revelation, the period of Domitian. Dr. Goodspeed sees it as the Roman Church's response to the challenge of Heb. 5:12 (see above, p. 96). The large use of the Epistles of Paul in this letter indicates a date at least as late as the nineties of the first century, when the work of Paul was first assembled and published.

[1] *Pliny Letters,* Vol. II (The Loeb Classical Library), pp. 401-7. The translations are by William Melmoth, revised by W. M. L. Hutchinson. Used by permission of Harvard University Press.

THE FIRST EPISTLE OF PETER

Not only the late date but also the style (1 Peter is written in almost the "best" Greek of the N.T.) will lead us to suspect that the Epistle was not written by Peter the Galilean fisherman and the later apostle. In all probability this is a case, like several in the N.T., of a later writer's addressing his contemporaries in the name of a revered leader who could not longer speak for himself. Readers of this series have already considered this kind of thing in connection with Ephesians. If, as is probable, this letter was written from Rome, the using of the name of the reputed founder of the Roman Church would have seemed thoroughly natural and appropriate.

See *ABC*, pp. 1338f., for a fuller introduction to this instructive and inspiring document of the ancient church in the period when it was first girding itself for its long war with the Roman state.

Reading 63: 1 Peter 1:1-12
THE PRIVILEGES OF THE CHRISTIAN

1. Using the last map in *ABC*, locate Pontus, Galatia, and the other provinces to which this Epistle is addressed. Notice that the major areas of Asia Minor are named in a kind of circular order in the salutation of the Epistle.

2. We have seen that this letter was written to encourage Christians threatened by, if not actually suffering, persecution. Note the verses in this section which refer, directly or indirectly, to that situation.

3. The mention of the "Dispersion" ("scattered") in v. 1 reminds us that the early church thought of itself as being the new (and true) Israel. The term was used to designate the Jews scattered abroad outside of Palestine. The same term is used in 1 Peter to describe the Christians, for they too are exiles from their true home (see Heb. 11:13f.).

4. Read the summary of the message of the Epistle, *ABC*, pp. 1339b-40a.

The author addresses the Christians of Asia Minor as "exiles" or "sojourners." This reminds us of Paul's remark,

"Our citizenship is in heaven," and of the statement in Hebrews to which attention has already been called. The early Christians were acutely aware of the fact that they did not belong to this world. Can you mention some of the points where the beliefs and practices of Christians in a pagan environment would have set them apart? How about the modern church and modern Christian? Are we probably not too much at home in the world as it is? Mention some of the respects in which we ought to be strangers and sojourners still. Is there not a sermon here?

It was easier for the first century (or early second century) Christians to realize that they were pilgrims on the earth, because they were being treated not as strangers only but as enemies. They were being subjected to actual persecution. The author begins his work of encouraging them in their trials by reminding them of the hope they have in Christ. Full salvation is yet to be realized, but even now they are "being kept" by the power of God for that salvation. And in it they can already rejoice. The readers of the Epistle have not seen the earthly Jesus, but they love him; and though they cannot see him with the eye of flesh, nevertheless even now they believe on him and rejoice in him "with joy unspeakable." In the same way we of today can love him and believe on him.

The section concludes with the reminder that this knowledge of Christ, revealed by the Spirit to the prophets but not fully understood by them, has been fully vouchsafed to the elect who are sojourners of the Dispersion. Even the angels might envy them their privileges.

Reading 64: 1 Peter 1:13–2:10
THE CHRISTIAN CHARACTER

1. With the help of a concordance find the places in the N.T. where Christ is compared with the cornerstone (cf. Psa. 118:22).

2. Read *ABC* on 1 Pet. 2:1-10 (pp. 1341*b*-42*a*). Can you not find a good sermon in the conception of the Christian

112

community as being a *living* temple, built around and upon Jesus? This same idea occurs in Eph. 4:16.

Having reminded the Christians of the wonder of their privileges, the author goes on to challenge them with their responsibilities. He begins: "Brace up your minds, then, keep cool, and put your hope for good and all in the grace that is coming to you at the revelation of Jesus Christ." This is Moffatt's translation of 1:13; and there is a sermon in it, especially for periods of great difficulty, when we are prone either to let our minds lag or to get confused. We are to be alert, but cool. We are to be holy—that is, belonging to God—remembering that God has purchased us (this is the meaning of "redeemed," 1:18) at an incalculable price, the death of his Son. The suggestion is that no one who remembers Christ's sufferings will be tempted to complain of the sufferings he may be called on to endure.

This holiness will express itself in the virtue of brotherly love and in the abandoning of all malice, deceitfulness, and quarreling.

The writer sees in Christ the cornerstone, precious to all who believe, but a stone to stumble over for those who do not believe. This is not far from the conception of Christ as both Saviour and Judge, as we have seen it in the fourth Gospel.

Observe the doctrine of the church in vv. 9-10. Christians form a new race, or nation, or people. This is the other side of the conception of "the sojourners." We are exiles on the earth only because our citizenship is in heaven.

Reading 65: 1 Peter 2:11–3:7
THE CHRISTIAN'S DUTIES

1. Read Rom. 13:1-7, noting the similarity of Paul's teaching on the proper attitude of Christians toward the Roman state to the same teaching in this Epistle.

2. The section 2:18–3:7, devoted to the duties involved in various household relationships, conforms to a well-known pattern. It is found in various Stoic sources and in

the N.T. at Col. 3:18f. and Eph. 5:22f. Compare these passages.

3. The Epistle to Philemon also throws light upon early Christian teaching about slaves. Read that also.

4. Would you agree with the writer, in vv. 19f., that patient suffering is more praiseworthy if one is being made to suffer unjustly than if one's sufferings are just?

This section begins with a general exhortation against self-indulgence. Christians must so live that non-Christians —that is the meaning of "Gentiles" (v. 12) here—will be impressed by their righteous conduct and won over to faith in God. The writer then proceeds to deal with the relationships of the Christians with one another and with others during this period of pilgrimage. They are to respect the legal rulers and submit to the government, except, of course (this appears elsewhere in the Epistle), when they are required to act in a manner inconsistent with their Christian faith, as, for example, when they are asked to offer sacrifices in a heathen temple or to the emperor's statue.

Slaves are to be submissive even to harsh and unjust masters. Do you think it is fair to cite the example of Jesus here? Note that the early church, although its message and life were utterly incompatible with slavery, made no deliberate effort to abolish that institution. No doubt, its vivid expectation of the end of this world with all its institutions and arrangements was in large part responsible for this attitude.

Women are so to live that if their husbands are not won to Christ by the message of the evangelists they may be won by the examples of their wives. The "immortal beauty of a gentle, modest spirit" (3:4—Moffatt) is a lovely phrase. Is there any justification for inferring from this passage that wives preceded their husbands into the church more often than husbands preceded their wives? Probably not; note that in 1 Cor. 7:12f. Paul deals with equal emphasis with the problems of the unbelieving wife and the unbelieving husband.

THE FIRST EPISTLE OF PETER
Reading 66: 1 Peter 3:8-22
SUFFERING FOR CHRIST'S SAKE

1. Does v. 13 conflict with the teaching of 2:19f.?

2. In v. 17 the author says: "It is better to suffer for doing right . . . than for doing wrong" (Moffatt). He obviously means more than "It is better to do right, even if one suffers, than to do wrong." What do you think of his position here?

3. Observe how close vv. 8-9—and indeed the Epistle as a whole, on the ethical side—are to the Sermon on the Mount in Mt. 5-7.

The tension between the Christian community and the society around in the period when this Epistle was written appears not merely in explicit references to persecution but also in the author's concern, expressed throughout, that Christians should live beyond all legitimate criticism. Here he indicates that one who acts justly and considerately will probably not be harmed; but if such a one is injured, let him bear his injury in such a way that, as Paul says, quoting from Proverbs, coals of fire will be heaped on his enemy's head. So one will be following the example of the Master, who suffered even unto death unjustly and for others.

One must be always ready to give an answer to anyone who wishes to know the basis for one's religious faith; but God can make more use of our *lives* than of our words. We must so *live* as to win over the unbeliever, and when we speak, let us be sure we do so with modesty and reverence. Here is something valuable for us as personal evangelists.

Vv. 19-20 are very difficult. This is probably a case where something has happened to the text in the course of early transmission, so that we do not have exactly what the original writer said. *ABC*, pp. 1342b-43a, offers some good light. Read those paragraphs in the Commentary.

Reading 67: 1 Peter 4:1-11
THE NEW LIFE

1. What light does this passage throw upon the question whether the readers of this Epistle had been Jews or non-Jews before their conversion to Christianity?

2. Note the illustrations of v. 4 given in *ABC,* p. 1343*a*.

One seems to hear an echo of Rom. 8 in vv. 1-2. Indeed, echoes of Romans are to be found in every part of the Epistle. Nothing is more certain than that its author was familiar with the Pauline letters.

The writer asserts that through the suffering of the body, borne with patience and discipline, one overcomes sin, and that thereafter one is able to live with a new righteousness, guided not by human desires but by God's will.

The readers are reminded of their past life. This is not to be taken necessarily as meaning that all of them had been guilty of the gross sins mentioned, unless an exception should be made of idolatry; but many of them had been.

It is an important and rather distinctive idea of this writer (another evidence of the lateness of the Epistle) that Christ went to preach to the spirits of the dead. We have observed this idea in 3:19f. Here it is stated again (4:6). (Is the same conception present in Eph. 4:9?) The conception seems to be significant for the writer in connection with the judgment of "the living and the dead." Can the dead be justly judged if the gospel is not first preached to them and if they are not given an opportunity to accept the mercy of God in Christ?

In v. 7 we are reminded again of how vivid and important in the church, even at the end of the first century, was the expectation of the end of this world.

The reference to "hospitality" in v. 9 brings to mind how large a part in the building up of the life and in the forging of the unity of the ancient church the custom of extending hospitality had. Christians from Corinth were assured a welcome in Rome, and travelers from Alexandria were certain to find friends and any needed aid among the Christians of Corinth or Ephesus. Read Rom. 16:1f. and Col. 4:10 in this connection.

Reading 68: 1 Peter 4:12-19
SUFFERING AS A CHRISTIAN

1. It is at this point that the letter of Pliny and the reply to Trajan quoted in the introduction (pp. 108f.) are particularly relevant. Read those letters again.

2. Read *ABC*, pp. 1343*b*-44*a*.

Some scholars hold that this Epistle is made up of two, or parts of two, letters of some early Christian leader. The argument is that whereas up to this point there have been a number of rather vague references to "tribulations," we have in the present paragraph a quite definite allusion to legal persecution. These scholars point to what they feel is a definite contradiction between this paragraph and 3:13 especially. Without necessarily agreeing with them, we can probably see some ground for this view.

Certainly vv. 12-19 were written with reference to a definite persecution situation. The Christians addressed are undergoing a "trial by fire." The writer urges that they should not fear or seek escape from suffering—suffering for Christ's sake is an honor—but that they should make certain that they are suffering *as Christians*. (You will remember that Pliny asks Trajan whether Christians are to be punished simply as Christians—that is, "for the name"— or only for crimes they may have committed.) In this connection it may be well to ask ourselves if we do not sometimes deceive ourselves into thinking that we are suffering for Christ's sake when really we are suffering because we are tactless or inconsiderate or foolish.

In vv. 17-19 the writer reminds his readers that when a Christian suffers unjustly and does not retaliate or take vengeance, one is not to suppose that injustice is being allowed to "get by." What is happening is that the Christian

117

is leaving the punishment of the wicked and the validation of the moral order to God, in whose hands are all things, including the punishment of all injustice and the vindication of the right.

Reading 69: 1 Peter 5
THE GOOD PASTOR

1. Would you gather from this passage that the persecution is local (that is, confined to Asia Minor) or happening also in other parts of the Empire?

2. In all probability the word "elders" in v. 1 refers not simply to older men but to the principal officers of the local church. Read in this connection pp. 141, 145, below.

3. Compare the reference to Babylon in 5:13 with Rev. 14:8.

4. Read *ABC* on this passage, p. 1344.

As the writer approaches the end of his Epistle, he turns to the leaders of the several churches, those who will be more responsible than anyone else for the actual inculcating of the lessons he has been trying to teach. Vv. 1-4 comprise a magnificent sermon on the Christian ministry—a sermon for ministers themselves.

First reminding his readers of the sufferings of Christ, who is later referred to as the "chief Shepherd," the preacher mentions three characteristics of the true shepherd, or pastor: he will be willing and glad, not grudging, in his service; he will serve not for love of pay but freely; he will not use his office to tyrannize the members of his church but will be an example of humility and love. Such a one will win a crown of glory in the presence of the chief Shepherd.

In v. 8 the note struck in 1:13 is sounded again. Moffatt says: "Keep cool, keep awake." Goodspeed renders it: "Be calm and watchful." This combination of poise and alertness is difficult and rare, but terribly important, especially in a day of stress and confusion like 1 Peter's—and ours. It is easy to be calm if one is not aware of what is going on;

and it is easy to become so thoroughly immersed in what is happening around one that one becomes as confused as the times themselves. And so this author keeps saying: "Be cool and calm, but stay awake!"

The Epistle ends as it began, with an assurance of triumph for those who are faithful even unto death.

Written Work.—The theme which more than any other engages the writer is the meaning of suffering. Gather together what he has to say on this theme and make a full outline of a sermon on this topic. A good title would be "The Christian Use of Suffering."

IV

THE EPISTLE OF JAMES

THERE are few, if any, documents in the N.T. concerning which so many contrary opinions have been held as about this little "Epistle" of James. I use the quotation marks because it appears to have been originally not an epistle at all but a sermon. It sounds very much like some early Christian pastor's message to his congregation, or excerpts from a number of his sermons, put into letter form for the purpose of more general publication.

One can ask hardly a single question about the Epistle and hope to receive anything like a unanimous answer from those who have seriously studied it. Even the *value* of the document has been questioned; most of us will recall Luther's famous characterization, "an epistle of straw." As to the time of writing, some (like Edward H. Sugden in *ABC*) make it out to be the earliest book in the N.T., dating it between 40 and 50 A.D. and thus even before Paul's letters; others place it much later, possibly as late as 125 A.D. As to destination, some (like *ABC*) regard it as having been addressed to Jewish Christians; others, to the whole church, Greeks as well as Jews. As to authorship, some (again like *ABC*) ascribe the Epistle to James, the brother of Jesus, who is known to have been prominent in the work of the Jerusalem church at the middle of the first century; others assert that we cannot know who "James" was but that he was certainly not *that* James.

It is not my purpose to enter into any discussion of these questions. The very fact that the Epistle is being considered in this volume of the Guide for Bible Readers series shows that I stand with probably the majority of contemporary N.T. students in regarding the document as one of the "later books." Some of the reasons for this position will appear in the comments on the text of the Epistle itself and do not need to be stated now. The only important element in the case for the early date is the claim of some that 1 Peter makes use of James; but the undoubted points of contact between the two documents can be explained just as plausibly, if not more so, by the assumption that James used 1 Peter as by the reverse claim. It goes without saying that if the Epistle is as late as 1 Peter its author could not have been James of Jerusalem, who is known to have become a martyr long before 1 Peter could have been written.

The Epistle itself gives us little indication of either time or place of writing. There is no reference either to persecution or to heresy in the ordinary sense. It is a sermon which might have been preached in any period—even our own. It thus serves to remind us that in the ancient church, as in the modern, much of the teaching work of the church proceeded without explicit reference to the special pressures under which the community might stand in a particular time and place. Often neglected, this Epistle has something of great importance to say to us, as it did to the ancient church. In many ways it is the most prophetic book in the N.T.

It is virtually impossible to make a satisfactory outline of this Epistle. It is a series of reflections on various subjects, and it is often not easy to see any logical connection between them. Someone has described the document as a "string of beads." That is a good description, especially if we remember that the beads are often genuine pearls.

Moffatt's Commentary on this Epistle (in *General Epistles,* Harper) is well worth adding to the list of books in *ABC,* p. 1330*b*.

Reading 70: James 1:1-18
THE CHRISTIAN UNDER TRIAL

1. Compare the salutation of James with that of 1 Peter.
2. Itemize the various topics dealt with in this *Reading*.

Do you see any connecting or unifying idea in the passage?

3. Compare vv. 2-4 with 1 Pet. 1:6-7 and Rom. 5:3-4. Jot down the outline of a sermon on tribulation as a character builder.

The author identifies himself as a "slave" of God and of the Lord Jesus Christ. Our familiar English version says "servant," but the Greek word is "slave," or "bondservant." Compare Rom. 1:1; Phil. 1:1; Tit. 1:1; Jude 1. These passages will indicate that the early Christians did not hesitate to describe themselves as God's, or Christ's, slaves. A good sermon might be preached on the appropriateness of that analogy: we have been bought and paid for (as slaves were); we have (ideally) subordinated our wills to God's; we have committed our future to him; we can rely only on his justice and mercy; and so on. It might also be pointed out that slavery to God is perfect freedom, that to be God's slaves means to be free from every human slavery, and that it is only by being a slave of God that one can be thus free.

"The twelve tribes which are of the Dispersion" would, if taken literally, be a reference to the Jewish dispersion—that is, to Jews living outside of Palestine. Actually it is an allusion to the Christian Church scattered over the world. The phrase reminds us again that the early church was likely to think of itself as the true Israel. The same idea is to be found, as we have seen, in 1 Peter, and often elsewhere. Thus, Edward H. Sugden in *ABC* is probably mistaken in his interpretation of this passage. (But see *ABC*, pp. 1328*b*-29*a*.)

In so far as there is any single conception binding the materials of this passage together, it is apparently the idea of the Christian under trial. ("Trial," A.S.V.—American Standard, or Revised, Version—mg., is a better translation than "temptation" in this passage, except for v. 14. Read *ABC*, p. 1331*a*, on the meaning of the Greek term here.) This is obviously the theme of vv. 2-4, and that theme is resumed in vv. 12-15. Vv. 5-11 and 16-18 appear to be digressions, the first suggested probably by the phrase "lacking in nothing" in v. 4, and the second suggested by the false charge that God may have sent temptation.

James is often thought of as being concerned only with the practical expression of the Christian life, not with its essential, inward character. That is true for the most part. But v. 18 reminds us that it is not altogether true. That verse might almost have been written by the author of the fourth Gospel.

Reading 71: James 1:19-27
PURE RELIGION

1. Read Mt. 7:21-23, comparing it with vv. 21-25. This is not the only passage in this sermon where one is reminded of the Sermon on the Mount.

2. Carefully read *ABC* on this passage, pp. 1332b-33a.

Again in this section the unsystematic ("string of beads") character of this Epistle appears, as indeed it does throughout. The author first urges self-control (we are to be quick to listen and slow to speak), and points out that man's anger does not work God's righteousness. (This is because man's anger, even when just, is never altogether disinterested; concern for self is mixed up with concern for justice.) There follows an exhortation, not clearly related to the preceding, that we strip ourselves "of everything that soils, . . . and of every evil growth" (v. 21—Goodspeed) and humbly receive the word which is able to take root in our hearts. The author proceeds to insist that receiving the word is more than merely listening to it; we must obey and practice it.

In an interesting passage the writer shows that he thinks of the perfect Law of God as being like a mirror, into which one cannot look without seeing how far from perfect one is. One who really "receives" the word will lay these imperfections to heart and will endeavor to get rid of them.

The passage ends with a repeated assertion about the importance of bridling one's tongue—a theme which the

123

writer will discuss yet again, and at greater length—and with a classical statement of how "pure religion and undefiled" will manifest itself. This familiar passage, which sounds so much like Mic. 6:8, reminds us that this writer is in many ways kin to the great prophets, especially of the eighth century B.C., with their concern for the poor and with their impatience with religious observances which covered all kinds of injustice, unchastity, and uncharity.

Reading 72: James 2:1-13
THE CHURCH AND THE POOR

1. In view of what was said about the meaning of "the twelve tribes which are of the Dispersion" in 1:1, what is probably the meaning of "synagogue" is 2:2? (This is the word rendered "assembly" in A.V.; see *ABC,* p. 1333*b*.) Are we to take it from the use of this Jewish term that the members of the churches addressed in this Epistle were necessarily Jewish?

2. In what kind of building would Christian assemblies in this period be held? See Rom. 16:5; 1 Cor. 16:19; Col. 4:15; Philm. 2; also Acts 19:9.

3. Would you gather from the passage that it was still true, as in Paul's time, that "not many wise, not many mighty" were called?

The word "have" in v. 1 of the A.V. means "hold," as it is rendered in A.S.V.; the author is denying the possibility of holding together faith in Christ, who is the Christian's only "glory," with attention to earthly rank or wealth. He goes on to show how such "respect of persons" sometimes shows itself even in the meetings of the Christians. Visitors would frequently attend the services (cf. 1 Cor. 14:23), and such outsiders are no doubt being referred to in this graphic story of the elegantly dressed man who is ushered to the best seat and the shabby fellow who is told to stand or to sit on the floor. This is not altogether ancient history, is it? Are not our churches often guilty of this same kind of obsequiousness toward the rich and contempt for the poor, sometimes quite as crudely expressed?

Vv. 6-7 show that this author uses the term "poor" as almost the equivalent of "pious." Compare the first beatitude in Luke (6:20) or Luke 12:21.

One thinks of the phrase "golden rule" when he hears "Thou shalt love thy neighbor as thyself" called the "royal law" (2:8).

In 10-11 the author makes the same point Paul insists on, although with a somewhat different purpose—namely, that one who is guilty of breaking one commandment is guilty of violating the whole Law. It is surprising that he selects such an example as murder. Surely none of the congregation would be guilty of that. Adultery, or covetousness, or even stealing, would have been far more likely. But the writer is only illustrating a principle.

This is the second time he has alluded to the "law of liberty" (see 1:25). That phrase represents his way of saying that although the Christian is no longer subject to the Law of Moses, he is subject to a higher Law, the Law of Christ. But this Law is an inward Law written in the heart, and obedience to it is therefore not slavery, as obedience to a merely external authority would be, but freedom.

Reading 73: James 2:14-26
FAITH AND WORKS

1. In connection with this passage read Gal. 3:1-9 and Rom. 4:1-12. Notice the similarity of literary style.

2. In the light of Rom. 4:13-17, can we take Jas. 2:21 as indicating that the writer and readers of this Epistle are Jews?

3. Would you say that this author is familiar with the letters of Paul and with Hebrews? If so, what does this indicate as to the date of his Epistle?

This, the most famous passage in this Epistle, well illustrates the most striking and engaging characteristics of its writer: his ethical earnestness, his interest in the practical and concrete, and his common sense.

The style is that of one of the Stoic preachers who were found almost everywhere in this period. These popular philosophers spoke on street corners or in the marketplaces and had an enormous influence on popular thought. They liked to speak as though they were carrying on an argument with some imaginary heckler or antagonist. Their sermons were filled with rhetorical questions and vigorous affirmations or rebuttals. It is doubtful that the thought of these Stoic preachers had any great effect on the N.T. writers, but their style undoubtedly did. One thinks of passages in Paul (such as those cited above, and others in his letters) and of a great part of the present Epistle. Passages can easily be found in Epictetus, one of the greatest of the Stoics, which read just like a chapter of James so far as style is concerned.

It is hard to escape the conclusion that James is speaking for the benefit of some contemporary group in which religious faith has become mere assent to certain formal beliefs, such as the belief that God is one. Its members may well have been appealing to Paul in urging that this assent was all that was required of them. James is not enough of a theologian either to understand Paul fully himself or to show that these people have misunderstood that apostle; he simply points out that their position is absurd: even the demons have that kind of faith. James is not denying the necessity of faith, but is insisting that unless good deeds accompany it faith is dead and futile. It is not difficult on the basis of a text from this little letter to show up the emptiness of many of our religious professions and observances.

Reading 74: James 3
THE CHRISTIAN TEACHER

1. Read *ABC* on this passage, p. 1335, observing especially the commentator's notes on the meanings of the several key words.

2. This passage is rich in sermon possibilities. Outline a sermon on "The Peril of Loose Talk," or "The Responsibility of the Christian Teacher," or "The True Wisdom." V. 17 is an excellent text for a sermon on the last of these topics.

Dr. C. H. Dodd in his book *The Apostolic Preaching and Its Developments* makes much of the importance in the early church of the distinction between preaching and teaching. Preaching was addressed principally to those outside the church and was evangelistic in purpose; teaching was concerned with the instruction and edification of the Christians themselves. The book of James is obviously a prime example of such teaching. It is not surprising, therefore, that the writer deals specifically with the duties and temptations of the teacher.

He begins by disclaiming any intention to urge people to become teachers. The teacher is in a position of greater responsibility and will be judged by a higher standard than members of the church generally. This reflection leads the writer to think of the power of the spoken word and of the irresponsibility with which this power may so readily be used. Talking is so easy, and yet so potent, whether for good or ill. The writer is more impressed, perhaps because of some personal experience, with the terrible *evil* a few words can so quickly do. The illustrations he uses—the fire in the forest and a poisonous plague—are telling and true. The suggestion that the tongue controls the whole body— as the bridle governs the horse and the rudder the ship—is not altogether convincing: as Moffatt suggests, we probably all have known reticent men who have learned to control their speech, but by no means their passions.

One must not suppose that in all of this discussion of the power of the tongue the writer is thinking only of the teacher. He doubtless has a more general application in mind. In the same way, in vv. 13-18, he is probably thinking of teachers principally, but also of others. One who

127

claims to be wise must prove his wisdom by his modesty
and his charity.

Reading 75: James 4
VARIOUS WARNINGS

1. Notice carefully the discussion of "lust" and "kill" in
ABC, p. 1336*a*.

2. Observe here (v. 5) a quotation from "Scripture"
which cannot be found in any known source. For Christians
of this period "Scripture" was more fluid than for us. The
N.T. canon had not been formed, and even what we know
as the O.T. did not have altogether fixed limits. The book
cited here was probably one of the works of Christian
prophecy, which were early regarded as having something
of the same value as the inherited Hebrew Scriptures.

This *Reading* deals with three topics, at first sight not at
all closely related. The first section, vv. 1-10, is a call to
penitence; the second, vv. 11-12, is an injunction against
censoriousness; and the third, vv. 13-17, is a warning against
forgetting that we are subject in all things to God's will.

The call to penitence is one of the most stirring in the
N.T. Notice how closely vv. 7-10 resemble the O.T. prophets. Apparently the sin for which repentance is particularly
called for is that of envy and quarreling in the church, a
matter touched on in the preceding section (3:13-18). Observe that the writer finds the source of quarreling and
conflicts among the brethren in inner cravings ("lusteth," in
the A.V., is too narrow a word to stand for the Greek term),
which are not subject to God's will. It was because Christians had worldly desires that they found themselves involved in this disgraceful competition and strife with one
another.

The warning against censoriousness toward others appears, on closer scrutiny, to be not unrelated to this
prophetic call to repentance. The first effect of penitence
is charity toward others' faults. One cannot be fully conscious of one's own sin and have any room left in one's mind

128

and heart for uncharitable faultfinding. Recall Jesus' parable of the publican and the Pharisee. The Pharisee, who finds so much fault with others, finds none with himself; the publican, who knows himself to be a sinner, says nothing about the sins of others.

The third passage is more detached in meaning—another "bead" on this string. The writer is warning against the presumption of those who forget God. This living as though God did not exist is what we mean by "secularism," and this ancient homily reminds us that secularism is no new thing.

Reading 76: James 5
FINAL EXHORTATIONS

1. Have you noticed that this Epistle contains very few references to Christ? List those which occur. Are there any in this passage? See *ABC* on vv. 6 and 11.

2. Do you feel that a statement like v. 15 needs qualification? How would you qualify it?

True to its general character, this Epistle ends with some rather miscellaneous exhortations. It is hard to discover any climax here to the Epistle as a whole. The final topic does not appear to have been chosen for that position with any particular purpose; thus the sermon seems to break off rather inconclusively.

In the first two paragraphs (vv. 1-11) the writer is again manifesting his sympathies with the poor and his resentment of their privileged oppressors. The statement of *ABC*, p. 1336b, that these oppressors were Jews is quite gratuitous. There is nothing to indicate whether they were Jews or not. Apparently they were not Christians—or certainly very few of them can have been—since in vv. 7-11 the author seems to identify the Christians with the poor.

In vv. 1-6 James speaks again in the tone of the great prophets, warning in effect, as Amos does, of the Day of the Lord as a day of retribution. The last sentence in v. 6 should probably read "Will he not resist you?" And correspondingly, in vv. 7-11, the writer urges the poor to be patient and steadfast, since they will not have to wait long for God's punishment of their enemies and his redemption of his "poor." Such a passage as this calls again to our minds the important fact that the early church had a much more vivid expectation of the coming judgment than we can have and suggests that the contemporary Christian preacher must take a position on social issues somewhat different from that of the ancient church leader. Do we not have to urge that God expects not only patience in the presence of social evil but action also?

The Epistle ends with teachings about oaths (very much like a sentence or two in the Sermon on the Mount), about prayer, and about the blessedness of the privilege of the teacher who leads a sinner to the truth.

Written Work.—Write a short essay on what seem to you to be the principal teachings of this Epistle, pointing out their modern value and relevance.

V

THE EPISTLES OF JOHN

IN addition to a Gospel of John, the N.T. contains three letters to which the name of John has been traditionally attached. The first of these (1 John) is a "general" Epistle in the sense that it is apparently addressed to Christians at large, although it should be added that, like Hebrews, the Epistle does not contain any formal salutation or address. The second (2 John) is a church letter, for we are undoubtedly right in taking "the elect lady and her children" to be a way of referring to a church and its members. (Cf. "She that is in Babylon, elect together with you" in 1 Pet. 5:13.) The third (3 John) is addressed to an individual named Gaius. Thus in these three letters we have a miniature letter collection of John, which, like the Pauline collection, contains letters of all three kinds: general, church, and personal.

Although scholars sometimes urge that 1 John is from a different hand than the other two, there are many reasons for believing that these three letters were written by the same individual. Who was that individual? He is not named in any of the letters, but 2 and 3 John refer to him as "the Elder." Now Papias, who was the head of the church at Hierapolis about 140 A.D., speaks of a "John the Elder," and it is usual to identify the author of the Johannine Epistles with this John. Similarities in style between the Gospel of John and these Epistles (especially 1 John) lead many to ascribe the Gospel also to the Elder (see *ABC,* p. 1065*a*). But these are all only conjectures. The identity of the author of the Epistles, as of the Gospel, must remain uncertain. The date and place of writing of the Johannine letters are also not clearly established, but it is usual to date the Epistles from 100 to 110 A.D., and to locate the author in Ephesus, and the churches for which he was responsible in Asia.

As to the occasion and purpose of the Epistles, one may say that they are aimed particularly at combating Docetism, about which I have spoken above (p. 19) and with which, as we have seen, the Gospel is also concerned. Be sure to read all that Professor Easton says about the theme of 1 John in his excellent introduction, *ABC*, pp. 1350f. We shall consider briefly the purpose of 2 and 3 John when we take up each letter in our *Readings*.

Reading 77: 1 John 1:1–2:6

LIFE IN THE LIGHT

1. After reading through this passage, jot down all the terms occurring in it which you can remember from the Gospel of John.

2. After reading *ABC* on this passage (pp. 1353-54) note all the phrases which reflect the author's awareness of the views of the Gnostic teachers.

It is hard to avoid the conclusion that the writer of the first few verses of this chapter was familiar with the Prologue of the fourth Gospel, if indeed he had not written it. There is the same emphasis upon Jesus Christ as the pre-existent Word of God, who was made flesh (notice the vigorous denial of Docetism in the statement that not only did the disciples see Jesus but they also actually touched him with their hands!) and thus became the revealer of God, the giver of light to men; there is the same stress upon Jesus Christ as the eternal Son of God, through whom we can have fellowship with the Father and share his life.

The passage is full of great texts. Vv. 7f. make one of these. What does John mean by living "in the light"? Does he mean living without sin? Or is the person "in the light" one who recognizes and confesses his sin? Such a person can be cleansed "of all unrighteousness" and can have communion with God. But one who (like many of the pretentious Gnostics) deceives himself into thinking that he has no sin—such a one walks in error and darkness and is shut out from forgiveness and from fellowship with God.

But though we must see and acknowledge our sin, we must not make peace with it. We are under obligation to keep the "commandments" of God, the chief of which is the commandment to walk as Christ walked (2:6). From this obligation the forgiveness available to us in Christ does not release us. On the contrary, the love of God for us expressed in Christ's sacrifice lays on us a heavier responsibility of obedience.

Reading 78: 1 John 2:7-17
THE LIFE OF LOVE

1. Compare v. 7 with Jn. 13:34, rereading the comments on the Gospel passage on pp. 69f., above.

2. Notice *ABC*'s explanation of how John can call the same commandment both "new" and "not new" (p. 1354a).

The phrase "new commandment" is so clearly reminiscent of the "new commandment" Jesus gave his disciples that it is difficult to resist the conclusion that vv. 7f. are, as *ABC* says, a kind of introduction to v. 9, where loving one's brother is made the heart and center of doing the will of God. You have noticed, in *ABC*, Dr. Easton's explanation of the sense in which this commandment is both new and old: it is new to the world in that it is given in Christ and in the church for the first time; but it is old to the Christian because he has known it since the very first moment he became a believer. Another way of understanding vv. 7-8 is to see in v. 7 a reference to the ancient Hebrew commandment to love one's neighbor as one's self. This commandment could hardly be called new, since it was present from the beginning; and yet it *is* new (v. 8), because its true meaning was not seen till it appeared in Christ.

Observe the phrase "in him and in you." The meaning

of Christian love is manifest not only in Christ but in the Christian. Indeed, could its meaning appear to the world "in Christ" if it were not also present in some measure in us? How unworthy we are of the phrase! And yet we cannot escape the responsibility it suggests.

Observe also the repetition in vv. 12-14, and read carefully *ABC,* p. 1354, on this passage. Vv. 15-17 make the transition to the succeeding section. We must not devote ourselves to securing and enjoying the things of this world, which is passing away, but to obedience to the will of God, who does not pass away.

Reading 79: 1 John 2:18-29
THE ANTI-CHRIST

1. Read *ABC,* pp. 846*b* and 1354*b,* and 2 Thes. 2:3-12 for background for this passage.

2. Would you say that this Epistle displays an attitude toward apocalyptic expectations different from that of the fourth Gospel? (See above, p. 72.)

It is clear that, late though this book is, its author has a lively sense of the imminence of the Second Coming. This is seen particularly in v. 18, where the "last hour" is spoken of, and in v. 28, where the Christians are urged to "abide" in Christ (cf. Jn. 15:4) in order that when he appears they may be ready and may not be ashamed. But it is seen also in the reference to "anti-christ."

A definite part of Jewish and early Christian apocalyptic was the belief that just before the end of the age and the appearance of the "Messiah," Satan would make a supreme effort to overcome the good and to forestall the victory of God and his Anointed. John here calls Satan "anti-christ," and he believes that this ruler of the realm of darkness is now making his final effort. He is making that effort through the Gnostic teachers, who are saying that Jesus the man was not also the Christ.

The position of these Gnostics, as of all Docetists, was that the divine Son of God could not actually have been a man.

134

They therefore either affirmed that Jesus' humanity was only an appearance—that he was a phantom—or else that the divine Christ took up his residence for a while in the body of a man, Jesus of Nazareth, but did not himself become human. To take either of these positions was, according to John, to "deny the Son" and to strike at the whole basis of the church's life and hope.

V. 19 tells us that the Gnostics have been driven out of the churches which are particularly addressed in this Epistle; but apparently their influence is still a threat to the church.

Reading 80: 1 John 3
SONS OF GOD

1. Would you say that the word "sin" is used in this chapter in a somewhat different sense from that in 1:8?

2. Jot down as texts for preaching vv. 2, 14, 17, and 22. There are other good texts in this rich passage.

The previous chapter ended with an allusion to the believer as "begotten of him." This conception of the believer as being in some literal sense the son of God is characteristic of this writer and of the author of the fourth Gospel. Notice Jn. 1:13 and 3:3-9 (*Reading* 7, above) and 1 Jn. 2:29; 3:12; and 3:9. In the Synoptic Gospels, the phrase "children of God" refers to a moral attitude and way of life: we are the "children of God" if our attitudes toward God and others are such as good children take toward their parents and toward one another (see Mt. 5:45). Paul's thought is much nearer to that of John, although he speaks of a new "creation" rather than of a new "birth."

Again, this writer insists that the mark of this new life is "love," especially love within the brotherhood. And he goes on to urge, in a manner reminiscent of James, that this love must be not in word only but in deed (vv. 17-18). The following verses (19f.) are difficult. Dr. Easton's interpretation (*ABC,* p. 1356*a*) is probably the best possible: John is warning against a certain kind of spiritual de-

135

pression. God is greater than our hearts and can overrule our own hearts' condemnation. This is one meaning of forgiveness. Since God has forgiven us, we must be willing to forgive ourselves. The proof that this forgiveness of God has been vouchsafed to us is the "Spirit which he gave us" (cf. Rom. 8:16).

Reading 81: 1 John 4
THE TEST OF THE SPIRIT

1. Carefully read *ABC*, pp. 1356-57, on this passage.

2. Observe how many of the ideas encountered already in our reading of this Epistle are brought together in this passage.

3. Can you think of a verse in Paul of which v. 9 is strongly reminiscent?

The reference to the Spirit in 3:24 leads the writer to recall that not everyone who claims to have the Spirit can be trusted. Some "prophets" are false. As *ABC* reminds us, Paul had proposed the formula "Jesus is Lord" as a test; John here, with the Gnostic teachers in mind, proposes "Jesus Christ is come in the flesh." The Synoptic Gospels assert that the false prophets shall be known "by their fruits." It will be interesting to set beside these biblical passages the following paragraph from a Christian manual of about the same date as 1 John, the *Didache:*

Not everyone who speaks in a spirit is a prophet, except he have the behaviour of the Lord. From his behaviour, then, the false prophet and the true prophet shall be known. And no prophet who orders a meal in a spirit shall eat of it: otherwise he is a false prophet. And every prophet who teaches the truth, if he do not what he teaches, is a false prophet. . . . Whosoever shall say in a spirit, "Give me money, or something else," you shall not listen to him; but if he tell you to give on behalf of others in want, let none judge him.[1]

[1] *The Apostolic Fathers*, Vol. I (The Loeb Classical Library), p. 327. The translation is by Lake. Used by permission of Harvard University Press.

The remainder of this chapter of 1 John is devoted to affirming and reaffirming the importance of love, especially love within the brotherhood.

Written Work.—Prepare a full outline of a sermon on "Christian Love," using as a text either vv. 7-10 or 19-20, being careful to deal with both the source and the fruits of Christian love.

Reading 82: 1 John 5
THE TRUE KNOWLEDGE

1. Read carefully the interpretation of the difficult v. 8 in *ABC,* p. 1357, noting also what is said there about v. 7, which is not found in the most ancient MSS.

2. Compare v. 13 with Jn. 20:31. Do you see any reason for calling vv. 18-21 "epilogue," as *ABC* does?

3. Notice what *ABC* says about the unpardonable sin, in commenting upon v. 16. In that connection recall also *Reading* 58.

This chapter is for the most part a summing up of the message of the Epistle as a whole. One after another of the characteristic ideas of its author appears here again: the crucial importance of believing that Jesus is the Christ; the fact that the believer is born of God, shares the sonship of Christ, possesses the divine life, has overcome the world; the Witness of the Spirit; God's readiness to answer the prayers of those who are living in accordance with his will. Attention is called to several new ideas in "Instructions" 1 and 3, just above.

The chapter—and the book—ends with three affirmations, each beginning with "we know." John is saying, "Here is the true knowledge, or Gnosis." Read *ABC* on this, p. 1358.

Reading 83: 2 John
A WARNING AGAINST HERETICS

1. Note the signs that the author of 1 John also wrote this Epistle.

2. Reread what was said about the Elder in the introduction, p. 131, above.

3. Note evidences that "the elect lady" is a church. Read *ABC*, pp. 1358-59.

It is clear at once that this little note, addressed to some unknown church, is concerned about the same Gnostic peril as is 1 John. Emphasis upon "the truth," and "the new commandment"; the definition of love as obedience to God's commands; denunciations of the Gnostic, who denies the humanity of Christ, as "anti-christ"—all these features belong also to 1 John. False prophets are again referred to in vv. 10-11.

There is no indication as to where the church addressed was located. If the Elder lived in Ephesus, it is natural to suppose the church was one of the churches of Asia.

Reading 84: 3 John
A LETTER TO GAIUS

1. Read the letter carefully and form your own independent judgment as to the occasion of it.

2. Do you think v. 9 could be a reference to 2 John?

This third Johannine letter is addressed to an individual, an unknown man named Gaius. We are not told in what relation he stands to the Elder, but we can assume that he was a leading member of one of the churches over which the Elder had supervision. The latter urges him to see to it that some "brethren"—traveling evangelists, perhaps—are well received by the church. Apparently on a previous occasion, when such brethren came, there had been trouble. Diotrephes, who is evidently in the position of greatest influence in the church—perhaps he was the bishop—had refused to receive them and had forbidden others to do so.

Demetrius is mentioned favorably, but as to how he is related to the Elder or to the church, we are not told. Read *ABC* (pp. 1359-60) carefully on this little Epistle.

VI

THE EPISTLES TO TIMOTHY AND TITUS

IN connection with 1 Peter we have had occasion to observe what is known as pseudonymity (see above, p. 111; and *ABC*, p. 1346*b*). In that case a Christian writer addresses the church in the name of a revered apostle, who can no longer speak for himself but who, it is felt, has something important to say to a later generation. There can be even less doubt that 1 and 2 Timothy and Titus are additional instances of this practice. (See *ABC*, p. 855*a*.)

To be sure, *ABC* (pp. 1274f.) takes the position that Paul probably wrote these letters, but that position has been more and more seriously discredited in recent years; and few scholars can now be found who defend the authenticity of these Epistles—that is, in their present form. Many would hold that fragments of genuine Pauline correspondence are embedded in them, especially in 2 Timothy (see *ABC*, p. 1275*a*). This is not the appropriate place to argue the question. The reader is referred to any of the Introductions mentioned on pp. 11f., above.

The very fact that the Epistles are being dealt with in this volume indicates the position which not only I but also the editor of the series take on this question. We regard the Epistles as belonging to a later generation than Paul's but as sincerely seeking to bring Paul's thought to bear upon certain pressing problems of that later time. Far from thinking it was unethical to use the Apostle's name, the writer may well have thought it would be unethical *not* to use it, when the ideas expressed were, in his opinion, all those of Paul. He may even have had some genuine

139

fragments or notes from Paul's hand as a basis for his work.

These Epistles are called the "Pastoral Epistles" because they are concerned so largely with pastoral problems. The names of Timothy and Titus are taken as symbols of all Christian pastors. Instruction is given on how the pastor's duties ought to be discharged, with special emphasis upon the danger of heresy and upon the qualifications of the various church officers who must lead the church's fight against it. What the writer has to say on these and other matters can be best observed in the course of our reading of the Epistles.

To the books on the Pastoral Epistles mentioned in *ABC* one may add E. F. Scott, *The Pastoral Epistles* (Harper); and R. Falconer, *The Pastoral Epistles* (Clarendon Press).

Reading 85: 1 Timothy 1
SOUND DOCTRINE

1. Note what the N.T. has to say about Timothy. See Acts 16:1-3; 17:14; 18:5; 19:22; 20:4; Rom. 16:21; 1 Cor. 4:17; 16:10; and so on.

2. Moffatt translates v. 5: "The aim of the Christian discipline is the love that springs from a pure heart, from a good conscience, and from a sincere faith." Here is the outline for a good sermon.

3. Notice that this *Reading* falls into four parts: vv. 1-2, vv. 3-11, vv. 12-17, and vv. 18-20. How would you formulate the topic of each section?

As has been at least hinted in the brief introduction, the major interest of the Pastoral Epistles is in "sound doctrine." This fact appears in the first sentence after the greeting of 1 Timothy (v. 3): Paul has left Timothy behind him in Ephesus that he might "charge certain men not to teach a different doctrine." Scholars have not been altogether successful in identifying beyond dispute just what was the false teaching against which the Apostle is made to give his warning. But there can be no question that, in general, it was Gnosticism, which existed in many forms and was able to appropriate and make use of materials of many sorts—Jewish, Christian, and pagan—for its purposes. Gnostic systems were featured by "fables and endless genealogies" (v. 4), and in other ways they suit the terms used in this Epistle and in the other Pastorals.

V. 15 introduces us to a formula often found in these letters: "Faithful is the saying." Each time the phrase seems to introduce a quotation from some familiar Christian source—perhaps from some early hymn that is lost.

The use of the word "faith" in v. 19 and elsewhere in this chapter (as in the Pastoral Epistles generally) is somewhat different from Paul's customary use of the term. For Paul, "faith" is personal trust in God and reliance upon his mercy alone; for the writer of the Pastorals, faith tends to be *the* "faith," that is, the "sound teaching" to which he so constantly refers. The objections of the Epistle of James on the subject of faith (see above, p. 126) would apply more fairly against the Pastorals than against Paul himself.

Reading 86: 1 Timothy 2:1–3:13
SOME RULES FOR THE CHURCH

1. Compare what the writer says about the conduct of women in the church with 1 Cor. 11:3f. and 1 Pet. 3:1f.

2. Consider carefully the rules about bishops and deacons in 3:1-13. Note down the qualifications. Do you regard them as wisely given? Observe that no reference is made at this point to the office of elder. This probably means that the terms "bishop" and "elder" were used to designate the same office.

After a digression (1:12-20) the writer returns to the main theme. In 1:3-1. Paul was reminding Timothy of what he had told him in Ephesus; now he goes on with some new instructions. The passage falls into two parts: one (2:1-15) dealing with the conduct of public worship, the other (3:1-13) with qualifications of bishops and deacons.

141

The exhortation that the Christians are to pray for the emperor and others in authority reflects the same attitude toward the state which we have noted in 1 Peter (and in Rom. 13). Notice the universalism implied in 2:3. The emphatic statement "There is one God" and the allusion to "one mediator" may well be by way of answer to the Marcionite belief in two Gods, one the Creator and the other the Redeemer (see above, p. 19), and to the Gnostic belief that between the highest God and ourselves were many "mediators." Marcionites and Gnostics also denied the reality of Jesus' humanity, as we have seen; this makes the forceful phrase "the man Christ Jesus" (A.V.) more significant.

The very conservative position taken on the matter of women's participating in the services will be judged less harshly if we remember that the important position which women undoubtedly had in the primitive Christian churches was in constant danger of being misunderstood in a period when women conventionally enjoyed very little freedom. V. 15 is difficult: does it mean that women can be saved only by giving birth to children? It is hard to believe the writer could have had any such idea. (How about Christian virgins?) Is it possible that we have here a reaction to the Marcionite teaching that marriage is sinful?

Reading 87: 1 Timothy 3:14–4:16
VARIOUS COUNSELS

1. Does 3:14 seem to you to be a natural explanation of this Epistle, or a part of an artificial setting? Read *ABC*, p. 1281*b*.

2. Notice the use of the word "faith." Does it conform to Paul's usage or to the usage we have already observed in this Epistle?

The writer now enters upon a series of rather miscellaneous counsels and injunctions for the Christian pastor. But first he indicates what is the ground for his concern about the work of the pastor by stating his view of the nature and importance of the church. The church belongs to the living God; it is "the family of faith"; it is the pillar and ground (Moffatt translates this word "bulwark") of the truth. This verse (v. 15) is obviously an excellent text for a sermon on the church.

V. 16 is usually identified as a stanza from an early Christian hymn, otherwise lost. It might also be a part of a primitive creed, or confession of faith. No doubt, as E. F. Scott points out, the crucifixion and resurrection were referred to in other parts of the original statement; but it is significant that "he who was manifested in the flesh" is so prominently included. This relation to "the flesh" was the point the Gnostics and Marcionites were denying.

The writer proceeds immediately to refer more explicitly to these "false" teachers, mentioning especially their ascetic practices. These practices, abstinence from marriage and from certain kinds of foods, were based upon the belief that this world is not the creation of God—that is, the true and highest God, the God and Father of our Lord Jesus Christ. Our author vigorously denies this vicious dualistic doctrine. God has made everything, and has made it for man's use and enjoyment; only let man use it properly, reverently, and thankfully!

The *Reading* ends with some important precepts for the pastor himself. He is to be careful about himself as well as about his teaching (4:16). The emphasis upon the necessity of discipline in the spiritual life is important, especially in the no less strenuous and dangerous times in which we live.

Reading 88: 1 Timothy 5:1-16
THE CARE OF WIDOWS

1. On the basis of this passage, set down the several kinds of practical difficulty the churches had apparently encountered in their efforts to care for the widows in their membership.

2. Do you think the church should now reaffirm the ancient custom of taking care of its own members who cannot support themselves?

This writer gives some excellent counsel to the young pastor as to how he should feel and act toward older men, younger men, and younger women. But he quickly moves on to deal at some length with widows, the care of whom apparently constituted a special problem for the churches he had in mind. He first directs that the churches should support only those widows who have no children or grandchildren to support them. (In this connection it is interesting to note an inscription on an ancient Christian tombstone in Rome, cited by Scott: "Erected by her daughter to the good Regina, her widowed mother, who lived a widow for sixty years and was never a burden to the church.") The author of 1 Timothy has some strong words to say to persons who refuse to support their widowed relatives.

A widow who receives support from the church is apparently expected to assume certain obligations of service. Young widows should not be included, because they are likely to remarry; indeed, the writer rather advises that they should remarry. (How different Paul's teaching on this matter!) The requirement that widows should be sixty years old was probably intended as a general rule, not to be adhered to too strictly. It is not likely that support would have been denied to a widow who needed it and who was qualified for it by her devout life, merely because she had not reached a designated age.

This passage reminds us of one of the most important factors in the triumph of ancient Christianity: it took care of its own. No Christian was dependent on public charity or the state. This fact was of the greatest importance, especially when, a little later, public charity began to fail and the Roman state entered upon its decline.

144

THE EPISTLES TO TIMOTHY AND TITUS

Reading 89: 1 Timothy 5:17–6:21

FINAL EXHORTATIONS

1. Notice the allegorical use of Deut. 25:4 here and in 1 Cor. 9:9. Where in "Scripture" is the sentence "The laborer is worthy of his hire"? What does this show as to the way the words of Jesus were regarded in the early church? The Gospels had probably not been canonized at this time.

2. Read again what Dr. Easton writes about church organization in this period in his Introduction to 3 John, *ABC,* pp. 1359f.

The way in which the elders are referred to in this passage and elsewhere in the Pastorals makes clear that the terms "elder" and "bishop" were applied indistinguishably and interchangeably to the highest officers of the local church in the period and area to which the writer of these Epistles belonged. In other documents of this same period—notably in the epistles of Ignatius—there are signs of a different kind of organization, the bishop belonging to a higher rank than the elders; but that is not true for these Epistles to Timothy and Titus.

The passage 6:1-2 reminds us of a passage in 1 Peter (2:18f.), not to mention Col. 3:22f. and Eph. 6:5f. Observe that this writer, like the earlier ones, makes no protest against the institution of slavery. On the contrary, Christian slaves are to serve their masters all the more faithfully because they are Christians and are to be, if anything, more obedient to Christian masters than to others. As always, this kind of exhortation is not far removed from a reference to the approaching end of the age (6:14f.).

The final paragraph of this Epistle points very specifically to Marcionism in the phrase "the oppositions of the knowledge . . . falsely so called," or, translated more accurately and literally, "the antitheses of what is falsely called 'Gnosis.'" Not only was Marcion generally accused of being a Gnostic; he also wrote a work, which the Marcionites held in high regard, called *The Antitheses.* In this work, which has not survived, Marcion apparently set what he conceived to be true Christianity over against Judaism, the religion of Christ over against the religion of the Law. Against this work and the Gnosticism which produced it, Paul (whom the Marcionites claimed as their own—see below, p. 156) warns the readers of this Epistle.

Reading 90: 2 Timothy 1
A PERSONAL APPEAL

1. Does v. 5 necessarily mean that Lois as well as Eunice had been *Christians* before Timothy? Does not v. 3 suggest an alternative meaning?

2. Vv. 7, 9-10, and 12 are excellent texts for preaching. Moffatt renders v. 14 in this striking way: "Keep the great securities of your faith intact."

3. Compare the use of the idea of being "ashamed" with Paul's use of it in Rom. 1:16-17.

Those who hold that the Pastoral Epistles, while not by Paul in their present form, nevertheless contain genuine Pauline materials can make their case most plausibly by an appeal to 2 Timothy, especially to chs. 1 and 4. No one who comes directly from 1 Timothy to ch. 1 of the second letter can escape the recognition that it reads much more like Paul than anything in the earlier Epistle. So far as *ideas* are concerned, there is scarcely a word in this chapter which the author of Romans, Corinthians, and Philippians might not have written; and even the stylistic and vocabulary peculiarities of the writer of the Pastorals are less conspicuous than in 1 Timothy or Titus—or, it may be added, than in chs. 2-3 of 2 Timothy.

Observe the approximation (closer than in 1 Timothy) to the usual Pauline form in the salutation; note also the "thanksgiving" (vv. 3-5), which is lacking in 1 Timothy and Titus. Certainly we have a right to say that this letter, if not more like Paul, is less unlike him. And the theory that genuine notes of Paul are embedded in it would explain the facts adequately.

146

Vv. 3-5 make an excellent text for a sermon on Christianity as a cultural climate or heritage, or on the place of the family in the church.

Reading 91: 2 Timothy 2
THE GOOD WORKMAN

1. Notice the "faithful saying" in vv. 11-13. Does it not sound as though it were a part of an early Christian hymn? Scott suggests that we compare it with Rom. 6:3f.

2. Does the inclusion of "of the seed of David" in v. 8 (a part of an early confession of faith, perhaps) suggest anything about the purpose of this Epistle? Would the Docetists or the Marcionites have used that phrase?

As we have seen, 1 Timothy is in no small part devoted to a description of the qualifications of those who will be the officers of the church. The second letter to Timothy contains little on this matter, probably because it is regarded as adequately handled in the other Epistle. Paul now says only that the officers should be "faithful," that is, dependable.

The writer then turns to Timothy himself, who is responsible for the church in Paul's own place. Vv. 3-6 emphasize the necessity of discipline and perseverance. This leads the writer to think of Paul's own trials, of the faith which sustained him in them, and of the purposes of God which were fulfilled through them. Moffatt renders v. 9b: "But there is no prison for the Word of God." Is there not a sermon here?

This passage contains a very sound warning against mere arguments, which often have the effect of confirming the skeptic, and even making new skeptics. Besides, arguments so easily become quarrels. The Christian preacher should rather, in gentle spirit, bear testimony to the truth, leaving to God the work of convicting men's minds and consciences.

The reference to the heresy of Hymenaeus and Philetus (vv. 17-18) that "the resurrection is past already" is difficult. Could they have been taking the position of the fourth Gospel (see above, p. 72), but without leaving any room at all for the final resurrection? So Scott suggests. Perhaps these teachers presumptuously believed that they had already entered an exalted spiritual state beyond the reach of sin, illness, and death. Gnostics were often thus deceived and thus deceived others. Can you think of modern sects which might in this respect be called "Gnostic"?

Reading 92: 2 Timothy 3:1–4:22
FINAL WARNINGS AND COUNSELS

1. Notice the way the Gnostic missionaries worked, as described in vv. 6-7. Is this only ancient history? Do not some modern Gnostic sects proceed by using similar methods?

2. Read *ABC*, p. 1287*b*, on 3:8-9.

3. Is it not clear that the time predicted in 4:3 had come when 2 Timothy was written?

As the writer approaches the end of his Epistle, he alludes to the "last days" (3:1), when sin will make a supreme effort to defeat God's good purpose. A long series of adjectives is used to describe those who will be Satan's agents in these "last days," which, it is clear, are, as the writer sees it, even now beginning. From among these corrupt persons come the Gnostic teachers who are now seeking to undermine the truth of the Gospel message.

This was true of many Gnostics, but not of the Marcionites, who practiced a high, even an ascetic, morality, as we have already seen. The emphasis (3:15-17), however, upon the importance and the inspiration of Scripture—this means what we would call the O.T.—would be appropriate against Marcionites as well as against a great many Gnostics, because their denial that the God of the Jews was also the God of the Christians led to a denial of the value of the Jewish Scriptures. Likewise, the emphatic affirmation that Christ will be the judge of the living and the dead was a repudiation of an important tenet of Marcionism. According to the Marcionites, the work of judgment would be done by the Creator God, not by Christ or his loving Father, who was concerned with redemption, not judgment.

Vv. 6-8 of ch. 4 are among the most memorable passages in the N.T. They make a wonderful text for a sermon on the life of Paul.

The personal references and directions with which the Epistle closes are interesting, but not helpful so far as the reconstruction of Paul's career is concerned. Even if authentic, they serve only to remind us of how sketchy our knowledge of Paul's life really is.

Reading 93: Titus 1
OPPOSING FALSE TEACHERS

1. Using a concordance, note the passages in which Titus is mentioned in Paul's letters. Observe that he does not appear in the Acts narrative.

2. Does Acts, or do the letters of Paul, refer to any activity of the Apostle in Crete?

3. Compare vv. 5-9 with 1 Timothy 3:1-7.

In this Epistle the author returns to the subject of the qualifications of the bishops, or elders; and again it is clear that his interest that these officers shall be worthy and able men grows out of his concern that the church shall offer effective resistance to the Gnostic heretics. Again, as in 1 Timothy, we get the impression that these heretics are making use of Jewish materials. As a matter of fact, Gnosticism in its many forms made use of the materials of all religions. The emphasis in v. 15 is probably to be placed on the second rather than on the first clause. The writer is probably using a familiar proverb in order to point the opposite moral: to men with perverted minds everything is unclean.

According to Clement of Alexandria and Jerome, the poet quoted in v. 12 is Epimenides of Cnossos. Is it credible that Paul or any other really sensitive early Christian writer could have referred to a whole nation in this way? Both Goodspeed and Moffatt render the last phrase of the quotation "lazy gluttons." Imagine a pastor working effectively among people whom he is able to think of and to characterize in any such way! Again, we are reminded that even the Bible does not altogether escape the marks of human error and sin. We must look *through* the words of men—never adequate and sometimes faulty—to Christ, who alone is the Word of God, made flesh.

Reading 94: Titus 2–3
FINAL INSTRUCTIONS

1. Notice the frequent use in this *Reading,* and indeed throughout the Pastoral Epistles, of the phrase "God our Saviour." Is this to be found in Paul's genuine letters? Consult the concordance.

2. Does the passage 3:4-7 sound to you especially like Paul? Jot down points of similarity and possible difference.

Titus is now informed about the kind of teaching he should be giving. Elderly men, elderly women, young women, and young men are severally addressed with appropriate counsels. The important virtues for this writer are temperance, fidelity to duty, seriousness, self-discipline; one misses the more adventurous virtues which Jesus or Paul would have included. Observe that the slaves are exhorted in terms not strikingly different from those which 1 Peter uses; and again note that this exhortation is not far removed from a reminder that Christ will soon come again to "redeem us from all iniquity" (2:13-14). Also the same attitude toward the state is enjoined as we have noted in 1 Pet. 3:1-2 and elsewhere.

Since the phrase "faithful is the saying" in 3:8 evidently to what precedes, vv. 4-7 are to be taken as a quotation from some unknown source. They constitute the religious high point of the Epistle and come near to representing the Pauline gospel. The whole passage, or v. 7 alone, is an excellent text.

Written Work.—Pull together some of the results of our reading of the later books of the N.T. by preparing a short essay (say a thousand words) on the meaning of "faith" in these books. Briefly characterize the positions of Hebrews, James, the fourth Gospel, and the Pastoral Epistles. The fourth Gospel does not use the word "faith," but it has much to say about "believing," which should throw light on the subject of the essay. These several views might usefully be compared with Paul's. See *Readings* 9, 58, 59, 73, and 85, above.

If you prefer, prepare a full outline of a sermon on "The Meaning of Christian Faith," showing that it is a rich, many-sided meaning to which these several N.T. writers make their distinctive contributions.

VII

THE EPISTLE OF JUDE AND THE SECOND EPISTLE OF PETER

THESE two short Epistles are commonly studied together for two reasons: first, they were written with a strikingly similar purpose; and, second, the greater part of Jude is actually reproduced in 2 Peter.

The common purpose of the two little letters is to combat a tendency to moral laxness and license which was threatening the life of the churches, at least in certain quarters. We have already seen that some forms of Gnosticism encouraged licentiousness by stressing the freedom of the initiated from the demands of the moral Law. And there were other sources of this fallacy, as Dr. Case points out in his admirable Introduction to 2 Peter in *ABC*. (Read especially under "Occasion," p. 1345.)

The authors of both Jude and 2 Peter are deeply troubled by this trend toward immorality, and they attack it fiercely. They do so not only by condemning all licentiousness as meriting God's anger but also by reaffirming the church's belief in the final judgment. This belief, one would gather especially from 2 Peter, had waned in strength with the passing of time, and indeed was being denied by some. Both writers, and especially the writer of 2 Peter, insist on the certainty of the judgment and warn all immoral persons of the destruction they must expect.

There are many indications that 2 Peter is almost, if not quite, the latest book in the N.T. Dr. Case gives an excellent summary of these indications on p. 1346 of *ABC*. Virtually all students of the Epistle date it about 150 A.D. or a little

later. No document in the N.T. is more surely pseudony-
mous.

The date of Jude is less certain. The fact that its contents
correspond so closely with ch. 2 of 2 Peter indicates that
one Epistle was based on the other; and since Jude is the
shorter it is natural to think of it as the earlier. But the
probabilities are that it is not *much* earlier. Read Dr. Case
on the date and authorship of Jude (*ABC*, p. 1361).

As to the place of authorship or the location of the
churches in whose welfare these writers were particularly
interested, we cannot know. The Epistles are addressed to
all Christians, and were probably intended for all who
needed their message, wherever they might be.

Reading 95: Jude
THE JUDGMENT OF GOD

1. Carefully read all that Dr. Case writes in *ABC*, pp.
1362f., about the structure and meaning of this Epistle.

2. Memorize the benediction, vv. 24-25.

3. Read Rom. 6:1f. for Paul's answer to an argument not
very different from that offered by some of Jude's opponents.

4. What does v. 17 indicate as to the date of this Epistle?

We gather from v. 3 that the author of this little "tract"
had planned a somewhat different kind of work: he had
intended to write an epistle on the meaning of salvation.
But growing evidence of the peril in which moral laxity,
encouraged by false and treacherous teachers, had placed
the church leads him to alter his plan and to address himself directly and only to this crisis.

The phrase "turning the grace of our God into lascivious-
ness" (v. 4) recalls a state of mind which Paul in Rom.
6:1*b* attributes to some of his opponents. His interpretation
of their attitude might be rendered thus: "Let us sin that
grace may abound. Since we are saved, not by obedience to
the moral law, but by the grace of God, it does not matter
what we do." This writer answers that the grace of God

does not destroy his judgment. He illustrates this fact from Jewish Scriptures, especially from the book of Enoch.

The paragraph in which Jude describes the false teachers, vv. 8-16, contains many interesting and striking phrases —as, for example, "[They] scoff at anything they do not understand" (Moffatt). Moffatt renders vv. 12b-13: "rainless clouds, swept along by the wind, trees in autumn without fruit, doubly dead and so uprooted, wild waves foaming out their own shame, wandering stars for whom the nether gloom of darkness has been reserved eternally."

Notice in vv. 3 and 20 that the word "faith" has the same general meaning as in the Pastoral Epistles.

Reading 96: 2 Peter 1-2
THE AUTHORITY OF CHRIST

1. Read Mk. 9:2f.
2. Carefully compare ch. 2 with the Epistle of Jude, noting the close parallelism.
3. Read *ABC* on 2 Pet. 2, pp. 1348f.

The writer devotes his first paragraph to a reminder of the nature of the Christian's calling and of the Christian virtues. The members of the church are urged to practice the virtues and thus make their "calling and election sure" (v. 10). In other words, even the believer is in danger of being excluded from the "eternal kingdom of our Lord and Saviour Jesus Christ" (v. 11b) if he neglects the moral obligations of the Christian life.

It will be remembered that Jude supports his position by appealing to the faith "once for all delivered unto the saints" (v. 3b). The author of 2 Peter makes the same appeal in a different way. He refers to the experience of the transfiguration as the evidence of the dignity and power of Christ and of the certainty of his coming again. It is interesting that this writer, alone in the N.T., appeals to the transfiguration rather than the resurrection (cf. Acts 2:32f.; Rom. 1:4) for this evidence. The point he is making is that the Christians can the more confidently expect to see Christ coming in glory because the Apostle and his associates have already seen him in that state.

V. 19*a* of 2 Pet. 1 means not that the words of prophecy are more sure than this experience of the Apostle himself but rather that these words are confirmed and strengthened by that experience. The predictions of the prophets (that is, predictions of judgment) are trustworthy—but not as they are interpreted by certain false teachers, who find their own private meaning in Scripture. Only authorized official teachers can be trusted to explain the prophets truly. This depreciation of the private interpretation of Scripture, as compared with that authorized by the community, is another indication of the late date of this Epistle.

Written Work.—Moffatt renders 1:5-8: "Make it your whole concern to furnish your faith with resolution, resolution with intelligence, intelligence with self-control, self-control with steadfastness, steadfastness with godliness, godliness with brotherliness, and brotherliness with Christian love." Fully outline a sermon on this text under some such title as "The Christian Character."

Reading 97: 2 Peter 3:1-18
THE CERTAINTY OF JUDGMENT

1. What do vv. 4 and 16 tell us about the date of this document?

2. Notice the addition to Psa. 90:4 which this author makes in v. 8. The second clause, in the sentence as it stands in 2 Peter, emphasizes the unimportance, from God's point of view, of a thousand years; the first emphasizes the vast significance, from God's point of view, of a single day. Is there not a sermon here?

It is not surprising that as the decades passed and the Lord did not return the early Christian hope of that event should have become less vivid. Some at the middle of the second century were apparently actually scoffing about it and were living as though there would be no judgment.

155

The writer here urges that just as the world has already been destroyed once, by water, so it will be destroyed again, by fire. He explains the delay by reminding his readers that God's sense of time is not the same as ours. He also points out that God is being patient with us, not slack. He wants to give all men every chance to repent. But the judgment will surely come—suddenly, swiftly, terribly—and we must live each day in readiness for it.

The reference to Paul in vv. 15f. shows not only that the letters of Paul have at this time been collected and widely published, but also that false and sectarian use is being made of them by certain interpreters. As a matter of fact, many Gnostics, and especially the Marcionites, made large use of the letters of Paul—and not always fairly. Marcion, having repudiated the Hebrew Scriptures, which were the only Bible the churches had till well after the middle of the second century, set up a new Scripture for his followers; and this new Scripture was in considerable part Paul's letters, somewhat abridged and modified to suit his theological views. It was some years later than this that the great body of the church created the N.T. and thus admitted the Gospels, Paul, and other apostolic works into the Christian Scriptures. We have, therefore, in the phrase "other Scriptures" in 2 Pet. 3:16 another evidence of the late date of this Epistle, for the letters of Paul were not generally regarded as Scripture till after 150 A.D.

No one, I imagine, would be disposed to claim that the books we have been examining and discussing in the course of the last twenty-five or thirty pages of this volume are among the greatest of the N.T. In one of his books C. H. Dodd makes a fruitful distinction between the books of the Bible which represent the insights of great inspired individuals and those which represent the efforts of communities to understand, assimilate, and make use of these insights. The last several Epistles we have read obviously belong in the second category, and their value consists largely in the light they throw upon the way in which the ancient church sought to meet some of the practical problems it confronted in the post-Apostolic Age. Such books are important not only for our understanding of early church history but also for the help they may give us in solving similar problems facing the church in our own period.

But though these books as a group do not stand among the most exalted books in the canon, the last verse of 2 Peter is an appropriate end of our reading and deserves a place among the great utterances of inspired Scripture. It suggests the prayer with which not only this volume but this series of volumes may well conclude:

May God bless our work together to our growth "in the grace and knowledge of our Lord and Saviour Jesus Christ." And "to him be the glory both now and forever. Amen."